COMBAT COLOURS
The de Havilland Mosquito
in RAF Fighter, Fighter Bomber and Maritime Strike roles 1942 - 1945

by Paul Lucas
artwork by David Howley

Contents

Part One:	Night Fighters, Intruders and High Flyers	P2
Part Two:	Fighter-Bombers	P24
Part Three:	Maritime Strike	P32
Part Four:	Mosquitoes in the Far East	P40

INTRODUCTION

The de Havilland Mosquito was one of the world's first true multi-role combat aircraft which could undertake a number of different roles with a high degree of success. During the Second World War it was used by the RAF as a Photographic Reconnaissance aircraft, Bomber, High Altitude Fighter, Night Fighter, Interdictor, Fighter Bomber and Anti Shipping Strike aircraft - and this only covers the broad role classifications, let alone the more specialised sub divisions of these roles.

This particular volume, Part Two of a two-part series, examines the camouflage and to a lesser degree the markings of Mosquitoes operating in the Fighter, Fighter Bomber and Maritime Strike roles. Mosquitoes operating in the Photographic Reconnaissance and Bomber roles were previously covered in Part One, **Combat Colours No 5 'The de Havilland Mosquito in RAF Photographic Reconnaissance and Bomber service 1941 to 1945'**.

Like the previous Mosquito volume, this volume draws on primary sources held by such institutions as the as the Public Record Office and RAF Museum amongst others, as well as a number of private individuals. These take the form of Air Publications, Air Diagrams, Air Ministry Orders; DTD Specifications; files once held by the Air Ministry, Ministry of Aircraft Production, Ministry of Supply, Royal Aircraft Establishment, Operational RAF Commands and Works Drawings. The result is not intended to be the final word on the subject, but aims instead to provide the aircraft enthusiast and modeller with a basic guide to what camouflage schemes and markings were carried by the Mosquito and why; and to provide a basis from which further research can be carried out.

The nomenclature used in this book is that of the documents consulted. Thus types of roundel are referred to by the correct terms used in Air Publication 2656A and other documents, not the Bruce Robertson notation familiar to most modellers. Proper colour names as given in various documents are begun with capital letters eg 'Ocean Grey', whilst colloquial names and references to a non specific colour, eg 'orange', are in small type throughout.

Paul Lucas

Acknowledgments

During the research for this book I have, as usual, received a great deal of help from a variety of people and institutions. Thanks are therefore due to:-
The Staff of the Public Record Office at Kew; the RAF Museum at Hendon; Birmingham Reference Library; Dudley Public Libraries; my sister Jane, brother-in-law Andy and *'Digger'*; Heidi Millington; Andrew Thomas; John Young AMRAeS; David Howley; and as ever the Combat Colours' Series Editor, Neil Robinson, who seems to be under the impression that sleep is optional!
Also as usual, any errors of fact or interpretation are mine alone.

Paul Lucas
Coseley
February 2003

Above: Mosquito nose - the end result of intruder sorties over enemy territory is graphically displayed on the nose of this, unfortunately unidentified, Mosquito NF II of 605 Sqn., circa 1944-45. The crudely applied individual aircraft letter 'O' and the fourteen *swastika* markings appear to be in Red. Sadly, the colour and precise nature of the artwork on the entrance door is unknown.

Scale Aircraft Modelling Colours
Combat Colours No.6
'The de Havilland Mosquito in RAF Fighter Bomber and Maritime Strike roles: 1942 – 45
by Paul Lucas
Artwork by David Howley
Series Editor: Neil Robinson
Design and layout: Steve Page
Published by Guideline Publications
352 Selbourne Road,
Luton, Bedfordshire LU4 8NU
Tel: 01582 505999
www.samnet.co.uk

Part One: Night Fighters and Intruders

As has been documented in Combat Colours No 5 **'The de Havilland Mosquito in RAF Photographic Reconnaissance and Bomber Service: 1941 to 1945'**, the first Mosquitoes to enter service with the RAF were the PR Is which joined the Photographic Reconnaissance Unit in July 1941, with the first Bomber Mosquitoes joining No 105 Sqn of 2 Group Bomber Command in November 1941.

By the time that these aircraft entered service, the Mosquito was also being developed as a fighter following the discovery that there was a requirement for both a modern Night Fighter and a long range convoy Escort Fighter. With the possibility of Mosquitoes becoming operational in these roles, on 26 January 1942, a meeting was held at the Air Ministry to attempt to come to some agreement about standardising the camouflage of Mosquito aircraft which might be used in similar roles by different operational Commands, each of which had different camouflage requirements.

The aircraft leaving the production line could be classified structurally as follows:-
* PRU/Unarmed Bomber
* Night Fighter/Fighter Bomber.

The roles of the aircraft in the first category were considered to be self explanatory, but those in the second category could be further divided as follows:-
* Night Fighter
* Fighter Bomber
* Intruder by day
* Intruder by night
* Escort Fighter
* Long range fighter.

Fortunately it was easy to agree that all Mosquitoes with a night role, ie Night Fighters and Night Intruders, should have the single colour scheme then in use for aircraft operating in both these roles - overall Special Night. This scheme had been adopted as the result of continuing efforts to find the best possible camouflage for night flying aircraft; a process that had its origins in the protracted trials ordered in December 1934 to try to find an upper surface camouflage scheme for use over the sea.

Camouflage for use at night

In October 1935, the RAE had begun trials of sea camouflage schemes in conjunction with Royal Air Force Coastal Area at the School of Naval Co-operation based at Lee-on-Solent to come up with a camouflage scheme to render the lower surfaces of Flying Boats less conspicuous when caught by a searchlight or flare during night operations. On 13 February 1936, it was suggested that Flying Boat under surfaces should be painted black. Whilst it was realised that this would make the aircraft more visible by day, concealment by night was considered to be more important. As a broadly similar view was held by the representatives of Air Defence of Great Britain who wanted a dark colour for the same purpose on the under surfaces of their new metal monoplane bombers.

The RAE carried out a whole series of tests over the next six months and finally produced a paint finish which offered not only low reflectivity, but was also quite durable. By 10 June 1936 the RAE received a letter which suggested that besides the under surfaces of aeroplanes, this new colour, now called Night, would also be convenient for the identification lettering on the camouflaged upper surfaces and as an overall finish on the airscrews. Thus Night was adopted as a standard camouflage colour and was in widespread service with Bomber Command as an anti-searchlight finish by the outbreak of war in September 1939.

This however, was not the end of the matter. A Professor T R Merton apparently thinking even better results could be obtained, went away and produced a *very* matt black finish using a material called optical black which would seem to be the material used to line the insides of items such as binoculars. Night absorbed 95 percent of the light falling on it, so any improvement in the finish must be in trying to reduce the remaining 5 percent.

However, at this time none of the aircraft camouflaged with the Temperate Land Scheme, which consisted of Dark Green and Dark Earth upper surfaces and Night under surfaces, were used *purely* as night bombers so any resulting improvement had to be suitable for *both day and night* operation. For this reason, the most obvious expedient, extending the Night finish up the fuselage sides and on to other parts of the airframe, was looked upon with disfavour because this would compromise the camouflage effect

Heading: Mosquito NF XIII, HK428, RO·K of No 29 Sqn., circa 1943-44. HK197 was built at Leavesden as an NF. XIII and was fitted with its radar on the production line which probably explains the matching camouflage demarcation line between the radome and forward fuselage. Note the standard mid-late war Night Fighter Scheme of overall Medium Sea Grey with Dark Green disruptive upper surface pattern and how the Red code letters have 'disappeared' into the Medium Sea Grey on the rear fuselage as has the lower part of the letter 'K' forward of the roundel.

of the Temperate Land Scheme by day.

Any improved finish would have to take in to account the need for such a finish to stand up to the wear and tear of service life whilst remaining aerodynamically smooth. Also a substantial reduction in the amount of light reflected in a *very* matt black finish, especially at high angles of incidence, would be possible if a small sacrifice in speed was considered worthwhile as this would reduce the chances of being seen and therefore the number of casualties.

Whilst this was possibly true for Bomber aircraft, this argument did not apply to Fighter aircraft - and as will become apparent, especially not for the Mosquito.

Experimental work at the RAE continued and by 15 June 1939, a new 'Special Dead Black' had been produced which had even greater light absorption. By mid-August trials of this new finish were being organised and had just started when the outbreak of war was declared on 3 September 1939. The trials were swiftly completed and found to be successful; and in September 1939, Special Night, as the colour was now called, was cleared for use by Bomber Command who were requesting that this material be adopted forthwith. Special Night was listed AP 1086 the Vocabulary of Stores under Stores Ref 33B/299.

Special Night

The first radar-equipped Night Fighters used by the RAF were Blenhiem Mk Ifs and Beaufighter Mk Ifs, originally camouflaged on their upper surfaces in the Temperate Land Scheme of Dark Green and Dark Earth to Air Diagram 1159. The Blenheims were originally Night on their under surfaces as they had originally been built as bombers, whilst the Beaufighters were Sky.

These finishes were not thought to be suitable for Night Fighter aircraft, so on 27 November 1940, Cypher X798 from the Air Ministry to all Commands at home and overseas specified that Night Fighters were to be painted black on all surfaces and to carry national markings as for Night Bombers. This was confirmed on 12 December by the issue of AMO A.926 which specified matt black on all surfaces. In the terminology of the time, the term 'matt black' appears to have meant Special Night 33B/299.

The reason that this Special Night finish was adopted for Night Fighters appears to have been poor searchlight control. Searchlights attempting to illuminate German bombers would, as often as not, accidentally illuminate a pursuing fighter instead, thus alerting the bomber whilst exposing the fighter to attack - either from the bomber it was pursuing or from anti-aircraft gunfire!

The solution to this would appear to have been to finish the Night Fighters in such a way as to make them as inconspicuous as possible under such circumstances by finishing the aircraft overall in the best anti-searchlight finish that it had been possible to devise, ie Special Night.

The overall Special Night finish remained in use throughout 1941 being cited in AMO A.513/41 issued on 10 July 1941, which stated, "Night Fighters are to be coloured matt black (special night) on all surfaces". National markings were to consist of Red and Blue roundels on the upper surfaces of the wings; Red, White, Blue and Yellow (1-3-5-7 proportioned) roundels on the sides of the fuselage and an equally divided Red, White and Blue fin flash. Serial numbers were applied in Red. This was the camouflage and marking scheme de Havilland's applied to the first production Mosquito NF IIs on the production line in the winter of 1941-42. This scheme is shown to advantage in the photograph of W4090, W4092 and W4088 which was taken at Hatfield in February 1942.

Roundel Modifications

Before any of the nocturnal Mosquitoes then taking shape at Hatfield could be delivered to the RAF, changes were being made to the identification markings of Fighter Command's Night Fighters. This came about mainly as a result of Bomber Command's experiences of having aircraft coned in searchlights over Germany. When this happened, the 1-3-5-7 proportioned Red, White, Blue and Yellow fuselage roundels were said to, "show up like lightbulbs", and thus make the aircraft easily visible. At the time this was thought to be because of the large proportion of white and yellow in the roundels and many squadrons made unauthorised modifications to their roundels in an attempt to combat this.

There was also some concern that the roundels were perhaps just a little too prominent in daylight as well, and as such, the problem was given an airing at a conference on the subject of aircraft camouflage held at the RAE which took place on 1 September 1941.

The head of the RAE's Chemistry Department, Dr Ramsbottom, felt that the problem with the searchlights was caused by applying the roundels to the ultra matt Special Night finished fuselage with standard Type 'S' paints which dried with a slight sheen. When illuminated, the Type 'S' paint used for the roundels reflected more of the incident light back towards the observer than the Special Night finish which diffused the incident light equally in all directions, thus making the roundel stand out.

As a result of the discussion of the problem it was decided to review the whole subject of roundels and fin markings with the aim of devising markings which, whilst remaining distinctive enough for identification purposes, were not more conspicuous than the aircraft which carried them. In meeting this aim, no change was to be made in the colours used, or the general form of the markings.

A further meeting was held to discuss the progress made so far on 24 October 1941, at which the suggestion was put forward that the best way of reducing

Below: Brand new Mosquito NF IIs, W4090, W4092 and W4088, photographed at Hatfield in February 1942, finished in the camouflage and markings called for by Cypher X798 of 27 November 1940. This was to consist of Special Night overall with national markings as for Night Bombers, with Red serials. Note how the upper wing roundels stand out by virtue of their Type S finish reflecting more of the incident light than the very matt finish of Special Night.

visibility by day would be to reduce the size of the white and yellow rings and to reduce the visibility by night by using a matt finish paint. The decision was therefore taken to produce a specific proposal for the narrowing of the white and yellow rings in the roundel and of the white band in the fin flash.

Action was swift and in November 1941, the RAE put forward its findings in report CN No 400 entitled, 'Note on identification markings of aircraft.' The report found that the fuselage roundel then in use consisting of a central red spot surrounded by concentric rings of equal width in white, blue, and yellow was visible on a dull day from more than a mile away. The full roundel effect could only be seen from about one third of a mile although the three outer rings could be seen separately at about half a mile.

Of the total amount of light reflected by the roundel, 1 percent was from the red, 31 percent was from the white, 3 percent was from the blue, and 65 percent was from the yellow.

The first idea tried out was to produce a roundel whose colours reflected an equal amount of light. The result was a marking which with an overall diameter of 4 feet would have a white ring of about 1 inch in width and a yellow ring of about half an inch in width. This gave a marking which was described as being unlike a roundel, instead resembling, "a wheel with a thin tyre and a small hub". It was considered unsuitable as a marking.

Because of this, an intermediate roundel which lay between the extremes of the roundel then in use and the equal reflectivity roundel was devised. The new roundel had ring widths in the proportions of red 6, white 1, blue 4, and yellow 1. When a roundel with a diameter of 4 feet to this design was tested on a dull day it was found to be visible for up to half a mile, thus being only about half as visible as the roundel currently in use. The roundel effect of the separate colour bands was visible at about one third of a mile, about the same distance as the roundel currently in use.

It was recommended that the new roundel be restricted to three sizes, 18 inches diameter for small aircraft, 36 inches for medium aircraft, and 54 inches for large aircraft.

Modifications to the fin flash were also considered, with modifications to the then standard 24 inch x 27 inch flash being carried out. Like the roundel, a flash which reflected equal amounts of light was considered unsuitable and an intermediate flash was also adopted in which a 2 inch wide band of white separated 11 inch wide bands of red and blue. This was found to have a visibility about equal to that of the new roundel.

As in the case of the roundel, it was recommended that the new fin flash be restricted to three sizes for small, medium and large aircraft. The width of the white band was to remain at 2 inches for all three sizes, with the flash being 18 inches square for small aircraft, 24 inches square for medium size aircraft, and 36 inches square for large aircraft.

The proposed changes to the roundels and fin flashes were submitted to the Air Ministry and on 21 January 1942, Fighter Command wrote to all its operational Groups informing them that the new markings were being adopted and instructing them to instruct all Night Fighter squadrons to apply them to their aircraft. The same letter also stated that the most appropriate colour for the squadron and individual aircraft code letters for Night Fighters had been found to be dull red and that therefore this colour should be universally adopted for Night Fighter aircraft.

Problems with Special Night
Even though the decision had been easily made to finish Mosquito Night Fighters in overall Special Night, the finish soon began to cause problems. On 27 January 1942, de Havillands wrote to the Directorate of Technical Development (DTD) at the Air Ministry to pass on the results of a test which had just been carried out on a Mosquito. De Havillands had carried out careful speed tests on one aircraft, (W4082), to determine what effect, if any, the application of the Special Night camouflage had on the performance of the aircraft.

At this time it was the accepted practice by all aircraft manufacturers to apply the Special Night camouflage in two stages. Firstly the aircraft was undercoated in Night paint before a second coat of Special Night was applied over the top. What de Havillands apparently did was measure the speed reached by W4082 when flown in just the Night undercoat, then apply the Special Night top coat and repeat the test.

What they had found was that when flown in the Night undercoat, W4082 had reached a true airspeed of 378 mph at an altitude of 22,000 feet and a weight of 17,000lbs., whilst the best the same aircraft could achieve when finished in Special Night was 352 mph - a loss of 26 mph!

When informed of this, the Controller of Research and Development (CRD) found this speed loss to be 'staggering' and immediately requested that the DTD check de Havilland's findings stating in no uncertain terms that if this indeed turned out to be the case, he wished the Air Staff to be made aware of the situation immediately and asking if they really required the matt finish for Night Fighters operating over the UK. CRD was of the opinion that searchlight control had now improved to the point where it was questionable whether the Air Staff would be right in insisting on the continued use of Special Night in view of the speed penalty incurred, and suggested that Night or Dark Green would be suitable instead.

Action on this matter appears to have been swift. Without waiting for the results of de Havilland's findings to be confirmed, the Directorate of Operational Requirements had contacted Fighter Command and appraised them of the situation. By 5 February 1942 C-in-C Fighter Command had agreed that the finish should be immediately changed from Special Night to what the documents dealing with this matter seen by the author refer to as 'smooth black', or alternatively 'smooth night finish'.

Below: Mosquito NF II, HJ911, photographed circa September 1942. HJ911 is finished overall in Night Type S known colloquially at the time as 'Smooth Night'. Note the sheen and reflection of the tail fin on the upper surface of the starboard tailplane and how the roundels on the upper surfaces of the mainplanes are almost indistinguishable due to the Night Type S reflecting as much of the incident light as the Blue of the roundel.

Smooth Night

Right from the introduction of camouflage paints in 1937, there had been some debate about the effect on aerodynamic smoothness of the introduction of the camouflage finish. During 1940, the original camouflage paints and dopes had given way to a new improved type with a much more finely ground pigment which resulted in a much smoother finish when sprayed on to an aircraft. No change was made to the specification numbers of the materials or indeed the colour, but the words 'Type S' were added to the title. By the end of 1940, with the exception of Special Night, all aircraft camouflage paints, whether Synthetic or Cellulose based, were supposed to be manufactured using type 'S' materials. The references made in primary source documents to 'smooth night' during early to mid-1942 are therefore almost certainly references to Night Type S.

Where references to 'Type 'S' materials are made, these should not be confused with the appearance of the letter 'S' on any airframe stencilling which might appear below a DTD number. The use of the letter 'S' below a DTD number when applied to the airframe signifies the use of a Synthetic as opposed to a Cellulose finish, which is signified by the use of the letter 'C'. Both Synthetic and Cellulose finishes could be made from the finely ground pigments which bestowed a type 'S' finish.

On 7 March 1942, the DTD wrote to the RAE to voice their suspicions that the excessive roughness of the Special Night finish which led to such a dramatic loss in performance of the Mosquito might be due to poor spraying technique. The DTD felt it was important to find out if this was actually the case, possibly, in the light of later developments, because the Special Night finish was widely used by Bomber Command. The RAE was asked to investigate.

On 14 March representatives of the RAE visited de Havillands where they were able to inspect Mosquito W4076 which was finished in Special Night. They found that the Mosquito had a surface finish which was considerably rougher than it should have been and considered that this was due to the dope having partially dried before reaching the surface. This resulted in a very rough finish with a loose powdery surface. The correct spraying technique was then demonstrated by the RAE representatives which involved flooding the surface with liquid paint which dried to a much smoother finish. If anecdotal evidence about the powdery nature of Special Night from Bomber Command is to be believed, de Havillands were not the only manufacturer to encounter problems in the spray finishing of their aircraft. Even as this was going on however, Fighter Command was petitioning for permission to undertake service trials of a new camouflage scheme of its own devising.

The problem of devising a suitable camouflage finish for Night Fighters was not new in 1941-42. Extensive trials to find a suitable camouflage scheme for night fighters had been carried out at Orfordness during the First World War as a response to the problems experienced by home based Night Fighters engaged in attempting to intercept first German airships and then bombers. Tactically, approaches to both types of targets tended to take place from below and behind so that the target was silhouetted against the night sky. Conversely, this meant that the approaching fighter would be viewed from above against the background of the earth's surface by the airship or bombers gunners, and it began to become apparent that some kind of specialist camouflage to make the fighter 'invisible' when viewed from above would be an advantage, especially on moonlit nights.

The task of devising a suitable camouflage was passed to the Ministry of Munitions Experimental Station at Orfordness where under the title 'Investigations into a Night Invisible Varnish (Orfordness)', various mixes of greys, greens, and blues were tested under varying weather conditions and different phases of the moon. As the project's full title was something of a mouthful, reports on the subject condensed it into the acronym 'NIV(O)' and eventually 'NIVO' which rolled off the tongue much more easily.

Developing a Night Fighter finish

After much testing a darkish grey-green hue which dried with a definite sheen was settled upon as giving the best results under average conditions. Orfordness report A/77 'Night Camouflage' of 1918, in summarising the state of the art, said that experiments over land and sea had shown that when viewed from above, aircraft treated with either a black or PC10 finish appeared as silhouettes, whilst aircraft treated with NIVO had, "......a distinct power of reflection which is apparently the same as the land and the sea". NIVO was therefore adopted as the standard upper surface colour for all night flying types from June 1918.

Between the wars however, the fact that NIVO had been developed for the upper surfaces of Night Fighters seems to have become lost, and NIVO became seen as an overall Night Bomber finish. When the camouflage trials of 1935 found it inferior to the new colour Night in anti-searchlight trials of camouflage for bomber aircraft, it shortly thereafter became obsolete. It is interesting to note that the 'power of reflection' was probably the reason it was found to be less effective in the early anti-searchlight trials mentioned above than Dark Green or Night, both of which had fully matt finishes.

Even so, not everyone appears to have forgotten about the original purpose of NIVO because on 28 November 1940, the day after Cypher X798 which introduced the overall Special Night scheme for Night Fighters was despatched, the Fighter Interception Unit based at Shoreham which was engaged in developing night fighting tactics and equipment, notified Headquarters Fighter Command that experience during the First World War had shown that dark green upper surfaces were superior to black and that suitable NIVO paint was still available at Farnborough. On 6 December 1940, Fighter Command agreed to a trial being carried out in which a Blenhiem was to be painted half black and half green, the colour demarcation running down the aircraft's centre line.

Once permission had been given, the FIU lost no time in implementing the trials, forwarding its report to HQ Fighter Command on 12 January 1941. It was reported that the trials aircraft had been painted black on the left hand side and green on the right hand side and then flown over both land and sea in bright moonlight. Observations were taken from another aircraft at a greater altitude than, and angles to, the target aircraft.

It was found that the green side of the aircraft was so inconspicuous over the ground that the Blenheim appeared to have only one wing, and that even over the bright moonlit sea, the green wing was less conspicuous. The report concluded that the dark green obtained from the RAE was a better upper surface camouflage for Night Fighters than the matt black currently being used.

Fighter Command were evidently not convinced as they asked for further trials to be carried out which proceeded over the next two months. When on 31 March 1941, the FIU forwarded a further report confirming its previous findings, Fighter Command authorised some service trials which were to be carried out by No 85 Sqn. Delays in these trials were experienced due to aircraft unservicability, but when the squadron finally submitted its report on 26 May 1941, it essentially confirmed the FIU's findings but stated that it thought the dark green was still too 'positive' and suggested a scheme of its own featuring a special colour mixed on the squadron.

At this point Fighter Command decided it needed to seek outside scientific help and sought to enlist the help of Sir Henry Tizard who had been instrumental in developing the Special Night finish for Bomber Command. Unfortunately, Tizard was not available and by 28 August, Fighter Command had been informed by the Ministry of Aircraft Production that further work on the camouflage of Night Fighters had been put in the hands of the Directorate of Scientific Research, and was to be carried out at Boscombe Down under the supervision of the RAE. In the light of this, Fighter Command was advised of a conference on aircraft camouflage being held at the RAE on 1 September 1941, which was being convened primarily to discuss the reports from the FIU and No 85 Sqn. It was suggested that representatives of both FIU and No 85 Squadron should attend.

At the conference, the RAE stated its view that such experimental work as was

5

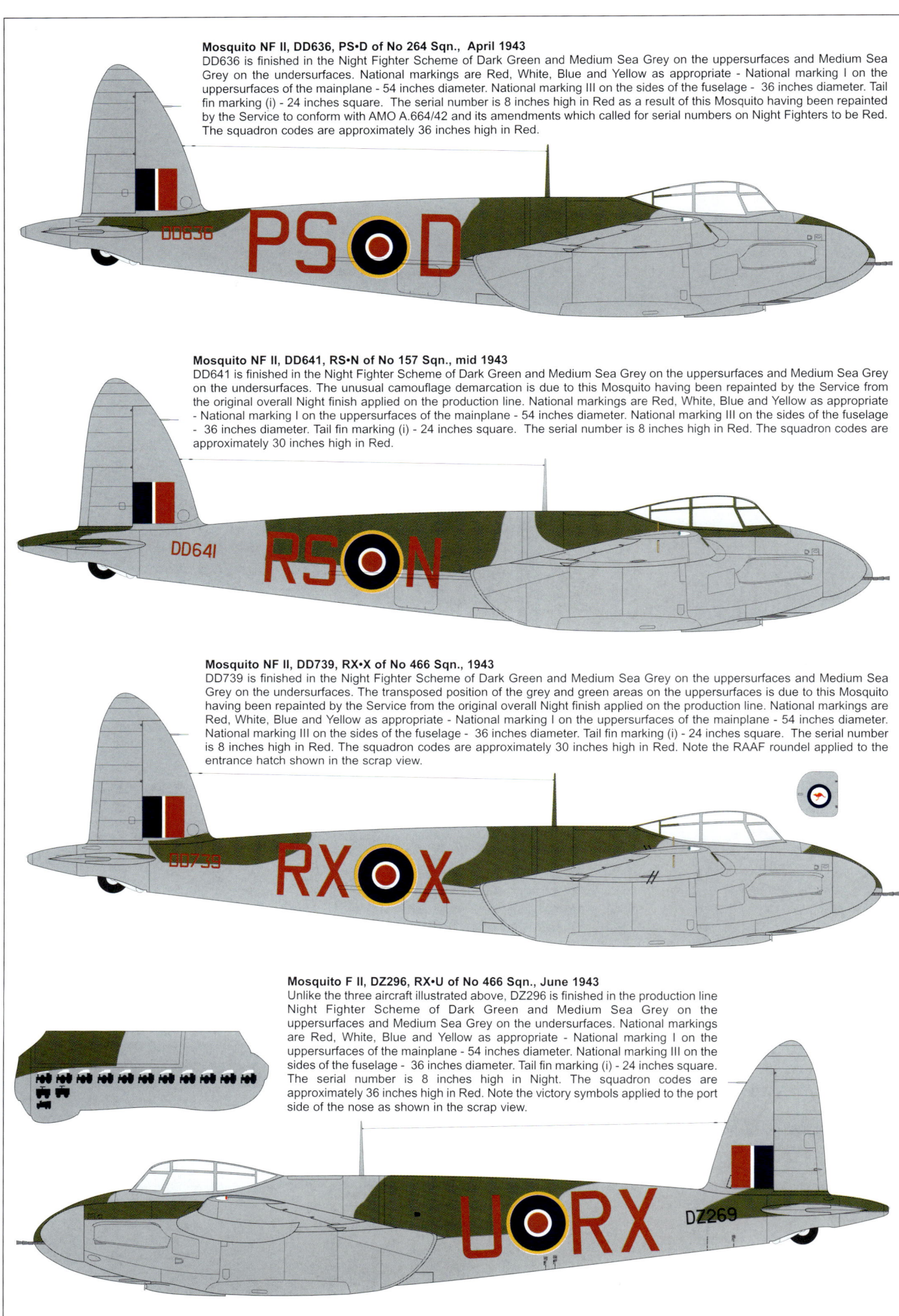

Mosquito NF II, DD636, PS•D of No 264 Sqn., April 1943
DD636 is finished in the Night Fighter Scheme of Dark Green and Medium Sea Grey on the uppersurfaces and Medium Sea Grey on the undersurfaces. National markings are Red, White, Blue and Yellow as appropriate - National marking I on the uppersurfaces of the mainplane - 54 inches diameter. National marking III on the sides of the fuselage - 36 inches diameter. Tail fin marking (i) - 24 inches square. The serial number is 8 inches high in Red as a result of this Mosquito having been repainted by the Service to conform with AMO A.664/42 and its amendments which called for serial numbers on Night Fighters to be Red. The squadron codes are approximately 36 inches high in Red.

Mosquito NF II, DD641, RS•N of No 157 Sqn., mid 1943
DD641 is finished in the Night Fighter Scheme of Dark Green and Medium Sea Grey on the uppersurfaces and Medium Sea Grey on the undersurfaces. The unusual camouflage demarcation is due to this Mosquito having been repainted by the Service from the original overall Night finish applied on the production line. National markings are Red, White, Blue and Yellow as appropriate - National marking I on the uppersurfaces of the mainplane - 54 inches diameter. National marking III on the sides of the fuselage - 36 inches diameter. Tail fin marking (i) - 24 inches square. The serial number is 8 inches high in Red. The squadron codes are approximately 30 inches high in Red.

Mosquito NF II, DD739, RX•X of No 466 Sqn., 1943
DD739 is finished in the Night Fighter Scheme of Dark Green and Medium Sea Grey on the uppersurfaces and Medium Sea Grey on the undersurfaces. The transposed position of the grey and green areas on the uppersurfaces is due to this Mosquito having been repainted by the Service from the original overall Night finish applied on the production line. National markings are Red, White, Blue and Yellow as appropriate - National marking I on the uppersurfaces of the mainplane - 54 inches diameter. National marking III on the sides of the fuselage - 36 inches diameter. Tail fin marking (i) - 24 inches square. The serial number is 8 inches high in Red. The squadron codes are approximately 30 inches high in Red. Note the RAAF roundel applied to the entrance hatch shown in the scrap view.

Mosquito F II, DZ296, RX•U of No 466 Sqn., June 1943
Unlike the three aircraft illustrated above, DZ296 is finished in the production line Night Fighter Scheme of Dark Green and Medium Sea Grey on the uppersurfaces and Medium Sea Grey on the undersurfaces. National markings are Red, White, Blue and Yellow as appropriate - National marking I on the uppersurfaces of the mainplane - 54 inches diameter. National marking III on the sides of the fuselage - 36 inches diameter. Tail fin marking (i) - 24 inches square. The serial number is 8 inches high in Night. The squadron codes are approximately 36 inches high in Red. Note the victory symbols applied to the port side of the nose as shown in the scrap view.

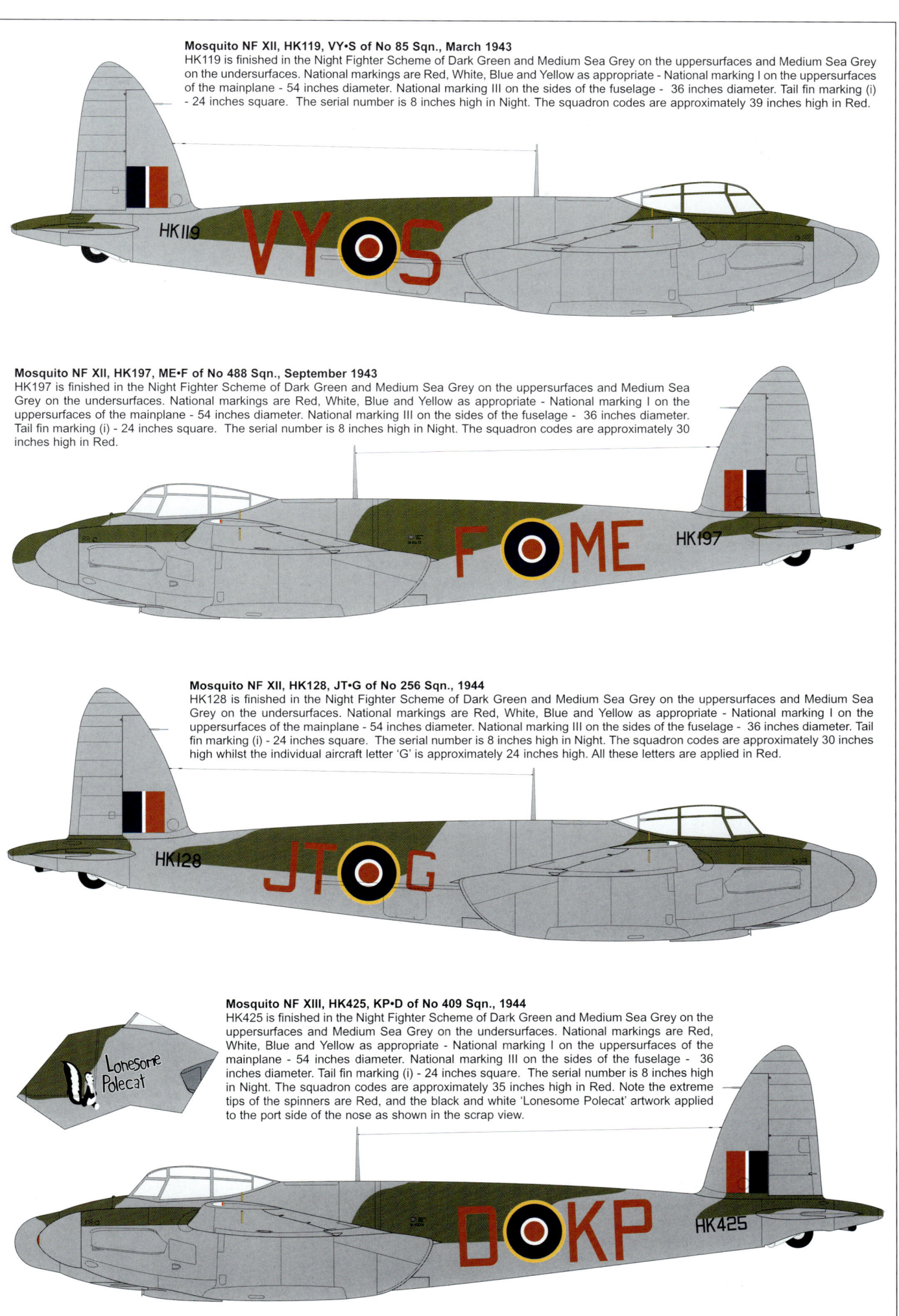

Mosquito NF XII, HK119, VY•S of No 85 Sqn., March 1943
HK119 is finished in the Night Fighter Scheme of Dark Green and Medium Sea Grey on the uppersurfaces and Medium Sea Grey on the undersurfaces. National markings are Red, White, Blue and Yellow as appropriate - National marking I on the uppersurfaces of the mainplane - 54 inches diameter. National marking III on the sides of the fuselage - 36 inches diameter. Tail fin marking (i) - 24 inches square. The serial number is 8 inches high in Night. The squadron codes are approximately 39 inches high in Red.

Mosquito NF XII, HK197, ME•F of No 488 Sqn., September 1943
HK197 is finished in the Night Fighter Scheme of Dark Green and Medium Sea Grey on the uppersurfaces and Medium Sea Grey on the undersurfaces. National markings are Red, White, Blue and Yellow as appropriate - National marking I on the uppersurfaces of the mainplane - 54 inches diameter. National marking III on the sides of the fuselage - 36 inches diameter. Tail fin marking (i) - 24 inches square. The serial number is 8 inches high in Night. The squadron codes are approximately 30 inches high in Red.

Mosquito NF XII, HK128, JT•G of No 256 Sqn., 1944
HK128 is finished in the Night Fighter Scheme of Dark Green and Medium Sea Grey on the uppersurfaces and Medium Sea Grey on the undersurfaces. National markings are Red, White, Blue and Yellow as appropriate - National marking I on the uppersurfaces of the mainplane - 54 inches diameter. National marking III on the sides of the fuselage - 36 inches diameter. Tail fin marking (i) - 24 inches square. The serial number is 8 inches high in Night. The squadron codes are approximately 30 inches high whilst the individual aircraft letter 'G' is approximately 24 inches high. All these letters are applied in Red.

Mosquito NF XIII, HK425, KP•D of No 409 Sqn., 1944
HK425 is finished in the Night Fighter Scheme of Dark Green and Medium Sea Grey on the uppersurfaces and Medium Sea Grey on the undersurfaces. National markings are Red, White, Blue and Yellow as appropriate - National marking I on the uppersurfaces of the mainplane - 54 inches diameter. National marking III on the sides of the fuselage - 36 inches diameter. Tail fin marking (i) - 24 inches square. The serial number is 8 inches high in Night. The squadron codes are approximately 35 inches high in Red. Note the extreme tips of the spinners are Red, and the black and white 'Lonesome Polecat' artwork applied to the port side of the nose as shown in the scrap view.

necessary would be best carried out under reproducible laboratory conditions. Based on work already done, it was thought that a grey upper surface camouflage would be better at all altitudes than the black currently in use, but that further experiments should be carried out to determine to what extent this was true under the different lighting conditions of a full moon; quarter moon; and starlight. This was quickly done as by the end of the month an internal RAE note concluded that any gain to be obtained by changing from black to any other colour was comparatively small, but the black scheme made the aircraft very conspicuous by day. However, a small advantage could be gained over the black scheme by using a dark green or grey which also had the advantage of rendering the aircraft less visible by day. No advantage was found to be gained by employing a disruptive scheme.

Fighter Command appears to have thought about these findings until January 1942, when it was decided that further service trials were to be held, this time by camouflaging the upper surfaces of one Flight of Beaufighters in 11 Group and a further Flight of Beaufighters in 12 Group, with a disruptive pattern of NIVO and a dark grey (matt finish). The matt finish referred to was the new Type 'M' finish which was just in the process of being introduced into service. This Type 'M' finish was to be as matt as Special Night, but available in a wider range of colours for use on the upper surfaces of night flying aircraft, especially Bombers.

On 21 February 1942 the DSR wrote to the RAE to inform them that the materials to be sent to Tangmere and Middle Wallop were to be Dark Green and Ocean Grey Type 'M' instead of NIVO and the dark grey because the colours had similar reflective properties and it would be preferable to use standard colours.

Whilst these service trials were being put in hand, the Mosquito NF II began to enter service with 157 Squadron with the first aircraft arriving on 9 March 1942. These initial aircraft in the W serial number range were finished in Special Night overall and retained the 1-3-5-7 proportioned fuselage roundels and equal proportion fin flashes. The serial numbers were Red. After delivery some attempt was apparently made to alter the fuselage roundels to resemble the new markings by overpainting most of the Yellow segment with Special Night. The fin flashes remained unaltered whilst the squadron codes and individual aircraft letter were correctly applied in Red.

It is thought that all the W-series Mosquito NF IIs which were delivered between January and March 1942 were finished in the Special Night scheme with the old style 1-3-5-7 proportioned roundels and that deliveries of Mosquito NF IIs in the 'smooth' Night scheme with the new roundels began with the first of the DD-series which started to be delivered from on or about 12 March 1942.

The Air Ministry promulgated the 'smooth' Night and other Mosquito camouflage schemes by Postagram on 6 March 1942 stating that, "Aircraft with a Night role are to be coloured smooth black on all surfaces and carry standard Night fighter markings".

The new roundels which had been introduced on Night Fighters in January 1942 evidently proved to be satisfactory, as on 30 April 1942, the Air Ministry wrote to all Operational Commands informing them that it had been decided that the modified National Markings and colour changes in the squadron and individual aircraft code letters had been approved for general introduction on all British Service aircraft.

The national markings were illustrated on Air Diagram 2001 which identified them as follows:-
The red and blue roundel - Type I
The red, white, and blue roundel - Type II
The red, white, blue, and yellow roundel Type III.

Over the next two years the types of roundels carried by both Day and Night Fighters remained fairly constant with the Type I roundel on the wing upper surfaces, and a Type III roundel on the fuselage.

The question of squadron codes
On 23 June 1942, the wisdom of continuing to employ the two letter code combinations which were painted on the sides of the aircraft to identify its parent squadron was called into question when the Deputy Director of Air Tactics at the Air Ministry wrote to Bomber, Fighter, Coastal and Army Co-operation Commands to inform them that it was now considered that the policy of applying these markings to the aircraft tended to 'stultify' all efforts to conceal the Order of Battle, and that unless the Commands could identify overriding reasons to the contrary, the use of the squadron codes would be abandoned. The views of each Command were sought as a matter of urgency.

Exactly what HQ Fighter Command thought of this idea is not known, but it would appear that a sufficiently strong case was argued for the retention of code letters because on 26 September 1942 the Air Ministry wrote to Bomber, Fighter, Coastal Army Co-operation Commands, the Middle East, India and West Africa informing them that it had been decided that with the exception of Bomber and Fighter Commands, all other Commands should dispense with this means of identification on security grounds.

Whilst being allowed to keep the two letter identification marking system Fighter Command was told that the squadron code letter combinations were to be changed at intervals of not greater than four months, and that these changes were to be staggered to confuse enemy intelligence. Despite this ruling, Fighter Command's Mosquito squadrons, once allocated their two letter code combinations, seem to have continued to use them for the rest of the war unchanged.

Trial results
By 21 July 1942, enthusiastic reports had been received at HQ Fighter Command from the squadrons involved in the service trials of the new Ocean Grey and Dark Green colouring for Night Fighters which was considered, "......infinitely more effective and preferable under all conditions of light and cloud......", and it was hoped that all Night Fighter aircraft would be painted with the new camouflage. The Air Ministry was informed of the findings of the trials by letter on 28 July 1942 at which time Fighter Command requested that arrangements be made to have all Night Fighter aircraft camouflaged with standard day camouflage on the upper surfaces, preferably over a lighter undercoat than was presently in use. Ten days later on 31 July, the DOR was able to reply to HQ Fighter Command to inform them that arrangements had been made for Night Fighters to be camouflaged in the standard Day Fighter Scheme to Pattern No 1 with Night undersurfaces.

The aircraft industry was informed of this change on 6 August 1942, by Amendment No 8 to DTD Technical Circular 144 which was entitled 'The Camouflage and Identification Marking of Night Fighters'. This stated that the DOR had ruled that Night Fighters were to be painted to the following scheme:- Upper surfaces Dark Green and Ocean Grey to the camouflage patterns of AD 1159 and AD 1160 as applicable; Under surfaces Night with the relationship between the upper and undersurfaces to be Pattern No. 1; Roundels, fin markings and serial number were to be in accordance with Air Diagram 2001 and spinners were to be Ocean Grey. No additional recognition markings were to be applied. The change was notified to the Service by Postagram the same day.

This however, was far from the end of the matter. On 16 August 1942 G/C Basil Embry at Wittering wrote a letter to the AOC 12 Group which criticised the new Night Fighter Scheme claiming that "The camouflage decided on by Headquarters Fighter Command is so wrong that it is difficult to believe that the matter has been given proper thought". Along with the letter, a report was enclosed on the results of experiments which had apparently been done first using model aircraft and then Mosquitoes under Embry's command which were a 12 Group initiative and had nothing to do with the official Fighter Command service trials mentioned above.

This defined the problem of camouflaging a Night Fighter as being primarily one of tone values. When observed in flight by an enemy, the fighter appeared as a solid dark object against a lighter background which varies in tone depending on the direction of approach taken by the fighter.

The most important point of the whole subject was seen as being that under all conditions the fighter became visible to the enemy as a dark object.

Right: Mosquito NF II, DD739, RX·X of 456 Sqn in March 1943. Originally delivered in overall Night, DD739 has been repainted in-Service to conform with the requirements of the Postagram of 11 September 1942 and AMO A.1096 of 8 October 1942, which between them introduced the new Night Fighter Scheme of Dark Green and Medium Sea Grey. Note and compare the transposed camouflage pattern with that applied on the production line and the Red serial number applied by the Service when compared with the Night serial number applied on the production line by de Havillands.

Below: Mosquito IIs, DZ717, UP·G and DZ714, UP·L of 605 Sqn., photographed circa March 1943, finished in the production Night Fighter Scheme with Red code letters and Night serial numbers on the rear fuselage.

Therefore if the fighter was painted black, the contrast between it and the background was intensified and the fighter would become visible at a much greater range than if the contrast were reduced.

The major conditions and backgrounds which were taken into consideration were:- clear sky; cloud; just below the horizon; and directly below.

If the fighter approached from above, and was therefore viewed against the sky, which even on the darkest night contains light, it would appear as a fairly strong silhouette. If it approached from below and was therefore viewed against the earth it would still appear darker than its surroundings as it was a solid object closer to the eye than the background which would be a considerable distance away, anything from several thousand feet, to 50 miles or more.

With the presence of cloud either above or below the fighter, the black finish increased the contrast with the background even more and there seemed little doubt that black was therefore the wrong colour or tone for a Night Fighter under any conditions.

Following all the tests and trials that had been carried out, the following conclusions had been reached.

Firstly, if the fighter should approach the enemy from a higher altitude than the enemy and would therefore seen above the horizon, the under surfaces and lower frontal area could not be painted too light a colour in order that the tone of the silhouette presented to the enemy should be reduced as near as possible to the tone of the sky which forms the background. Irrespective of how light the frontal area and under sides were painted, the aircraft was bound to pass through a stage when it would be visible as a silhouette, but it would be more difficult to see than if it were painted black, and afterwards it would once again tend to melt away into the background.

Secondly, if the fighter approached from slightly below the enemy and was therefore seen just below the horizon it would be viewed against a background which whilst darker than the sky above would still be lighter than that provided by the ground below. With the frontal area painted white and toned down by the scarcity of light coupled with the reflected light of the sky from the fighters upper surfaces; the light coloured camouflage would be at its most efficient.

Finally, if the fighter approached its target from below where it would be seen against the comparatively dark background of the earth, the upper surfaces of the fighter should be camouflaged in a similar way to those of day fighters only be a little bit lighter. This would compensate for the fact that the background was considerably further away.

12 Group passed this report on to HQ Fighter Command where it apparently joined other critical comments which would seem to have been made about the decision to finish the undersurfaces of Night Fighters finished in the new scheme in Night. An internal Fighter Command memo dated 18 August 1942 comments that the original reason for finishing the undersurfaces in Night was to reduce the visibility of the fighter if it was illuminated by searchlights, and that all the deliberations on the subject of Night Fighter camouflage that had recently taken place had been directed at the uppersurfaces only.

The Night Operations staff at all Fighter Commands operational Groups had been consulted on the matter and all felt that it would be better if the undersurfaces of Night Fighters were camouflaged with light grey. The recommendation was therefore made that the undersurfaces of Night Fighters should be grey and this was accepted by the AOC in C Fighter Command on 23 August.

On 25th August 1942, Fighter Command redefined the finish it wished to be applied to night fighters as follows:
• Upper surfaces were to be Dark Green and Sea Grey Medium
• The under surfaces, fin, rudder, and spinners were to be Sea Grey Medium
• National markings were to be as detailed in AMO A.664/42, and no further tactical fighter markings were to be carried.

The under surfaces were defined as all surfaces below a line from the centre of the nose to the centre of the tail of the fuselage passing through the leading and trailing edges of both main and tailplanes. Where either the main and or tail planes were positioned above or below the centreline of the fuselage the boundary between the upper and under surfaces was to be curved in the appropriate direction to the centre of the fuselage.

No sooner had this been done than the Air Ministry and MAP queried it. Was it really necessary to change the colour of the upper surfaces yet again? On 31 August, Fighter Command replied that after all the time and trouble which had

Mosquito NF XIII, MM555, KP•B of No 409 Sqn., December 1944
MM555 is finished in the Night Fighter Scheme of Dark Green and Medium Sea Grey on the uppersurfaces and Medium Sea Grey on the undersurfaces. National markings are Red, White, Blue and Yellow as appropriate - National marking I on the uppersurface of the mainplanes - 54 inches diameter. National marking III on the sides of the fuselage - 36 inches diameter. Tail fin marking (i) - 24 inches square. The serial number is 8 inches high in Night. The squadron codes are approximately 30 inches high in Red. MM555 carries the remains of almost a full set of the black and white distinctive markings associated with Operation Overlord as called for by SHAEF Operational Memorandum No. 23. Each black or white band was 24 inches wide. By the time the photograph on which this illustration is based was taken, some attempt had been made to remove the markings from the uppersurfaces of the wings as sanctioned by Amendment No. 3 to SHAEF Operational Memorandum No. 23 of 19 August 1944. The black stripes however, remained visible.

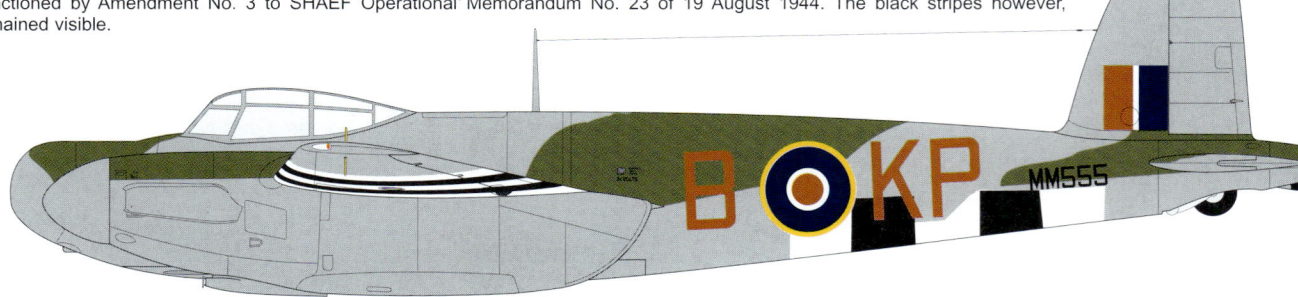

Mosquito NF XXX, MM767, RA•U of No 410 Sqn., circa winter 1944/45
MM767 is finished in the Night Fighter Scheme of Dark Green and Medium Sea Grey on the uppersurfaces and Medium Sea Grey on the undersurfaces. National markings are Red, White, Blue and Yellow as appropriate - National marking I on the uppersurfaces of the mainplane - 54 inches diameter. National marking III on the sides of the fuselage - 36 inches diameter. Tail fin marking (i) - 24 inches square. The serial number is 8 inches high in Night. The squadron codes are approximately 30 inches high in Red. MM767 still carries the 24 inch wide black and white distinctive markings associated with Operation Overlord on the undersurfaces only as called for by Amendment No. 3 to SHAEF Operational Memorandum No. 23.

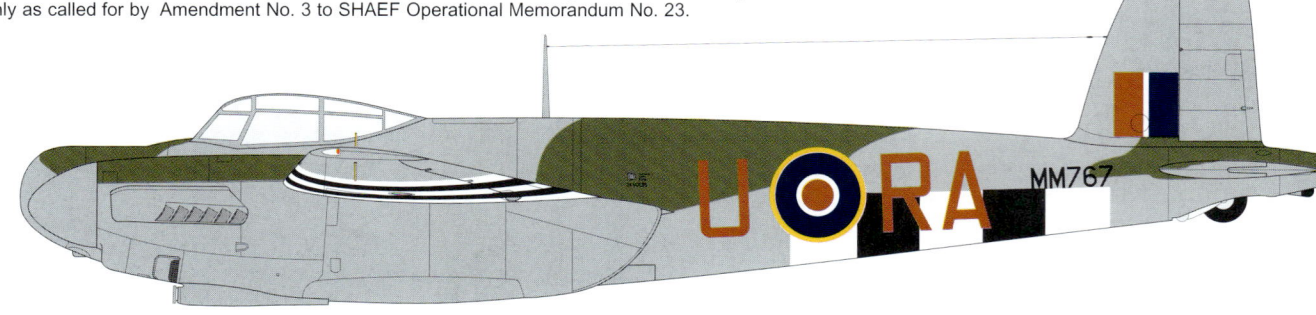

Mosquito NF XIX, TA446, RS•Q of No 157 Sqn., January 1945
TA446 is finished in the Night Fighter Scheme of Dark Green and Medium Sea Grey on the uppersurfaces and Medium Sea Grey on the undersurfaces. National markings are Red, White, Blue and Yellow as appropriate - National marking I on the uppersurfaces of the mainplane - 54 inches diameter. National marking III on the sides of the fuselage - 36 inches diameter. Tail fin marking (i) - 24 inches square. The serial number is 8 inches high in Night. The squadron codes are approximately 30 inches high in Red. The individual aircraft letter 'Q' is repeated as an approximately 6 inch high character which is thought to be Yellow with a thin Night outline.

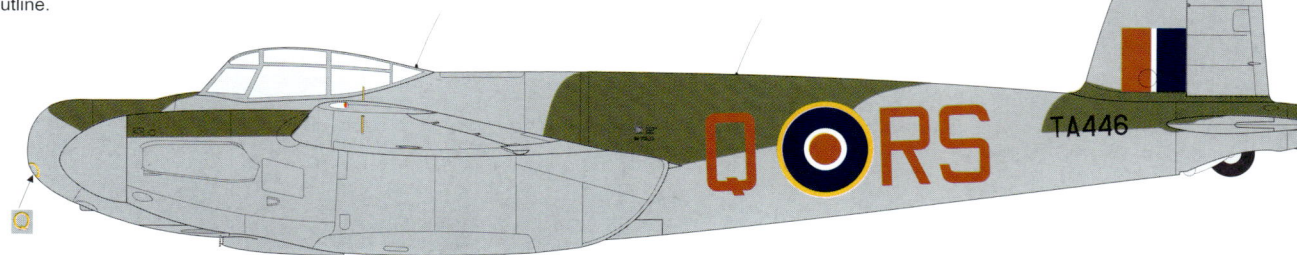

Mosquito NF XXX, NT264/G, RX•R of No 466 Sqn., May 1945
NT264/G is finished in the Night Fighter Scheme of Dark Green and Medium Sea Grey on the uppersurfaces and Medium Sea Grey on the undersurfaces. National markings are Red, White, Blue and Yellow as appropriate - National marking I on the uppersurfaces of the mainplane - 54 inches diameter. National marking III on the sides of the fuselage - 36 inches diameter. Tail fin marking (i) - 24 inches square. The serial number and '/G' suffix which denoted an aircraft which was to be guarded at all times when away from its home base are 8 inches high in Night. The squadron codes are approximately 31 inches high in Red.

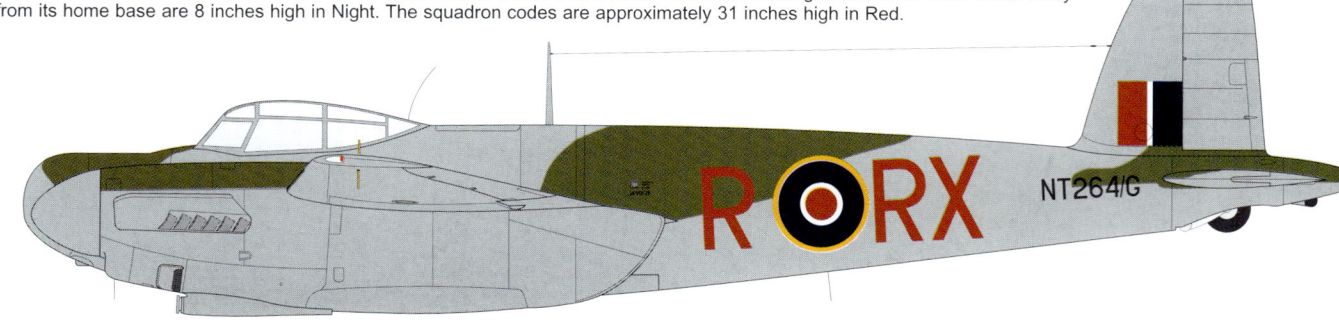

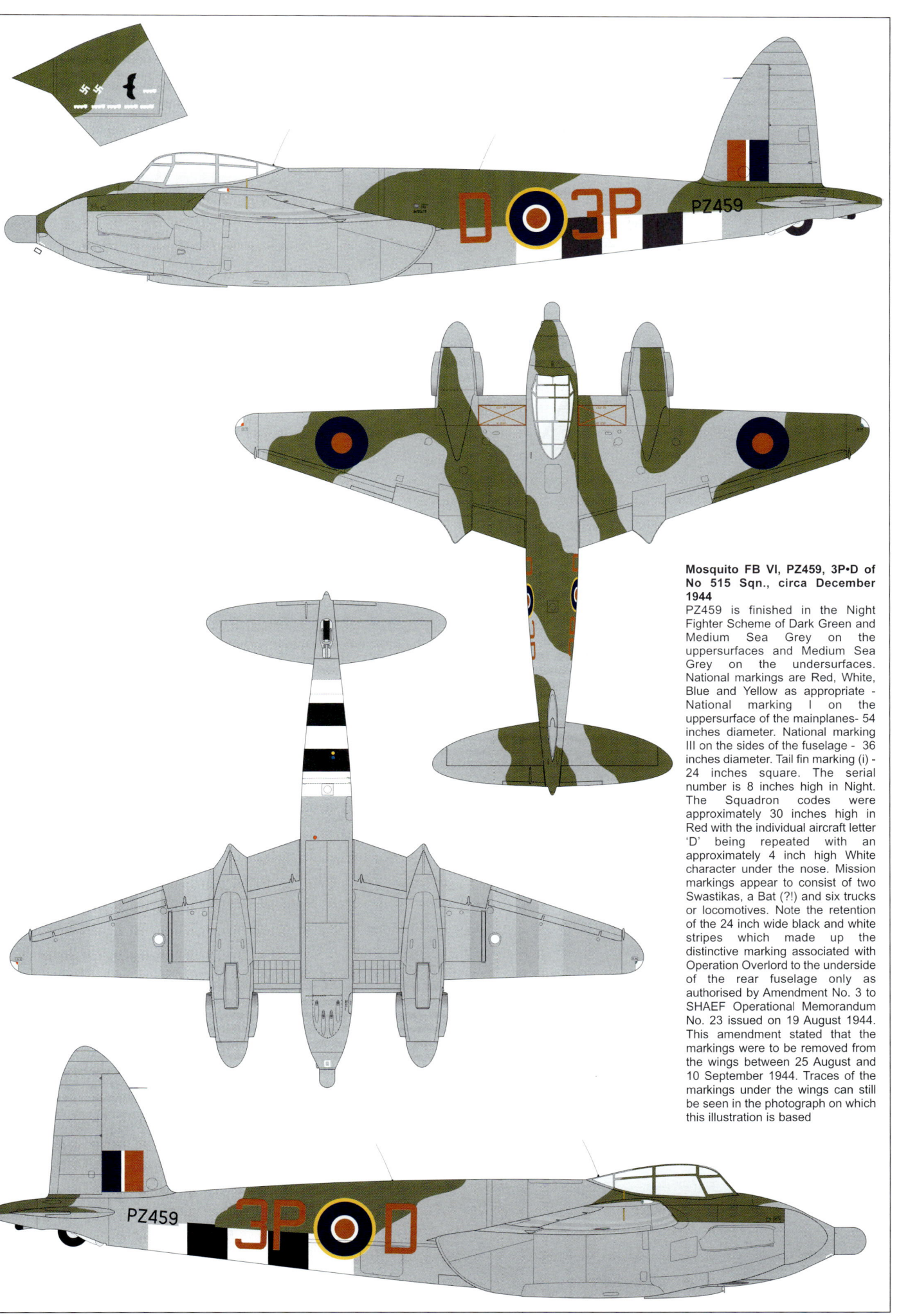

Mosquito FB VI, PZ459, 3P•D of No 515 Sqn., circa December 1944

PZ459 is finished in the Night Fighter Scheme of Dark Green and Medium Sea Grey on the uppersurfaces and Medium Sea Grey on the undersurfaces. National markings are Red, White, Blue and Yellow as appropriate - National marking I on the uppersurface of the mainplanes- 54 inches diameter. National marking III on the sides of the fuselage - 36 inches diameter. Tail fin marking (i) - 24 inches square. The serial number is 8 inches high in Night. The Squadron codes were approximately 30 inches high in Red with the individual aircraft letter 'D' being repeated with an approximately 4 inch high White character under the nose. Mission markings appear to consist of two Swastikas, a Bat (?!) and six trucks or locomotives. Note the retention of the 24 inch wide black and white stripes which made up the distinctive marking associated with Operation Overlord to the underside of the rear fuselage only as authorised by Amendment No. 3 to SHAEF Operational Memorandum No. 23 issued on 19 August 1944. This amendment stated that the markings were to be removed from the wings between 25 August and 10 September 1944. Traces of the markings under the wings can still be seen in the photograph on which this illustration is based

Left: Mosquito NF XII, HK197, ME·F of 488 Sqn., circa October 1943. HK197 was originally built at Leavesden as a Mk II in May 1943 but was converted in to an NF XII by Marshalls of Cambridge who fitted the centimetric radar in the 'Thimble' nose radome visible here. Note the mismatch between the Dark Green on the radome and the Dark Green on the forward fuselage at the joint between the radome and fuselage.

Below: Mosquito NF XXX, MM813, FK·H of 219 Sqn circa 1944/45. The NF XXX was the ultimate Mark of Mosquito Night Fighter to see operational service during World War Two. MM813 was taken on charge by 218 MU on 23 August 1944 in the standard Night Fighter Scheme with the only additions to the markings made by the Service being the Red squadron code letters which were applied by the Squadron. Note the two stage Merlin engines and the large flame dampers on the exhausts.

gone into devising this scheme, they would not settle for anything less and on 11 September 1942, the new Night Fighter scheme was promulgated by Postagram before being included in AMO A.1096 dated 8 October 1942. It is interesting to note that AMO A.1096 made no change to the Service requirement for the serial number to be applied in Red which led to aircraft repainted in the new scheme by the Service having Red serials, whilst aircraft which were manufactured in the new scheme had Night serials, possibly a legacy of the short-lived instructions to finish Night Fighters in the Day Fighter Scheme.

Intruder camouflage

Up to this point, the camouflage scheme applied to Intruder aircraft had been identical to that of Night Fighters, ie overall Special Night or Night, and the new Night Fighter Scheme was only intended to be for Night Fighters. Whether it was by coincidence or not is not known, but sometime around the end of August 1942, HQ Fighter Command's Air Commodore Night Operations paid a visit to No 23 Squadron at Manston

whose Mosquitoes which were finished in overall Night, were engaged on Intruder operations over occupied Europe, and the camouflage of the aircraft came up for discussion.

It was arranged for a trial to take place to compare an aircraft finished in the new Night Fighter Scheme with one of 23 Squadron's overall Night finished aircraft to asses the new scheme's suitability for Intruder Operations. The trials were carried out at Bradwell Bay on

Below: Mosquito NF XIII. HK425. KP·R of 409 Sqn., in the spring of 1945. HK425 serves to illustrate how the Night Fighter Scheme did not change between its introduction in 1942 and the end of World War Two. HK425 was completed at Leavesden in November 1943 in the Night Fighter Scheme with National marking I on the upper surfaces of the wings, National marking III on the fuselage and Tail fin marking (i) on the fin. The serial number is applied in Night and the Squadron codes and individual aircraft letter have been added by the Squadron in Red.

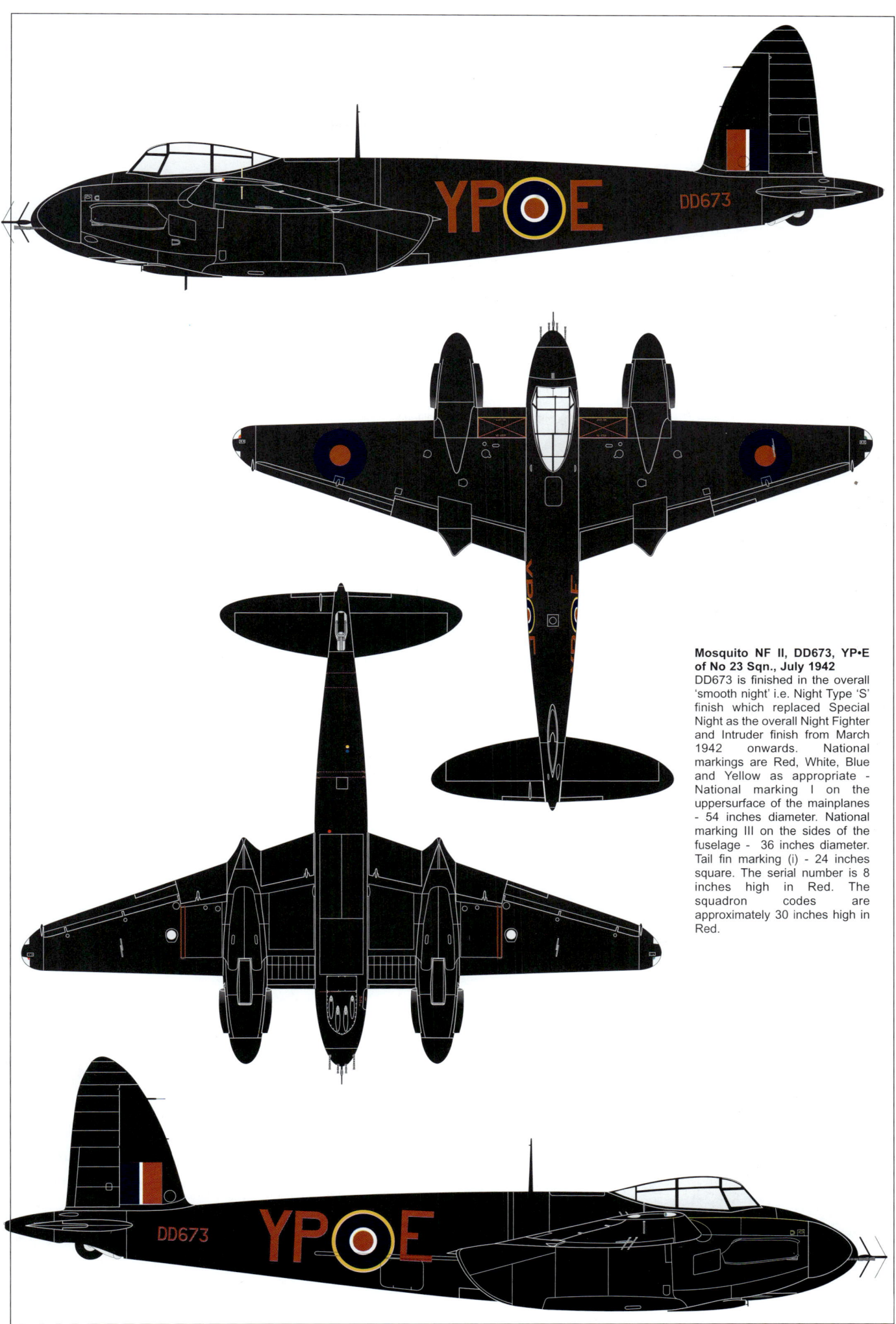

Mosquito NF II, DD673, YP•E of No 23 Sqn., July 1942

DD673 is finished in the overall 'smooth night' i.e. Night Type 'S' finish which replaced Special Night as the overall Night Fighter and Intruder finish from March 1942 onwards. National markings are Red, White, Blue and Yellow as appropriate - National marking I on the uppersurface of the mainplanes - 54 inches diameter. National marking III on the sides of the fuselage - 36 inches diameter. Tail fin marking (i) - 24 inches square. The serial number is 8 inches high in Red. The squadron codes are approximately 30 inches high in Red.

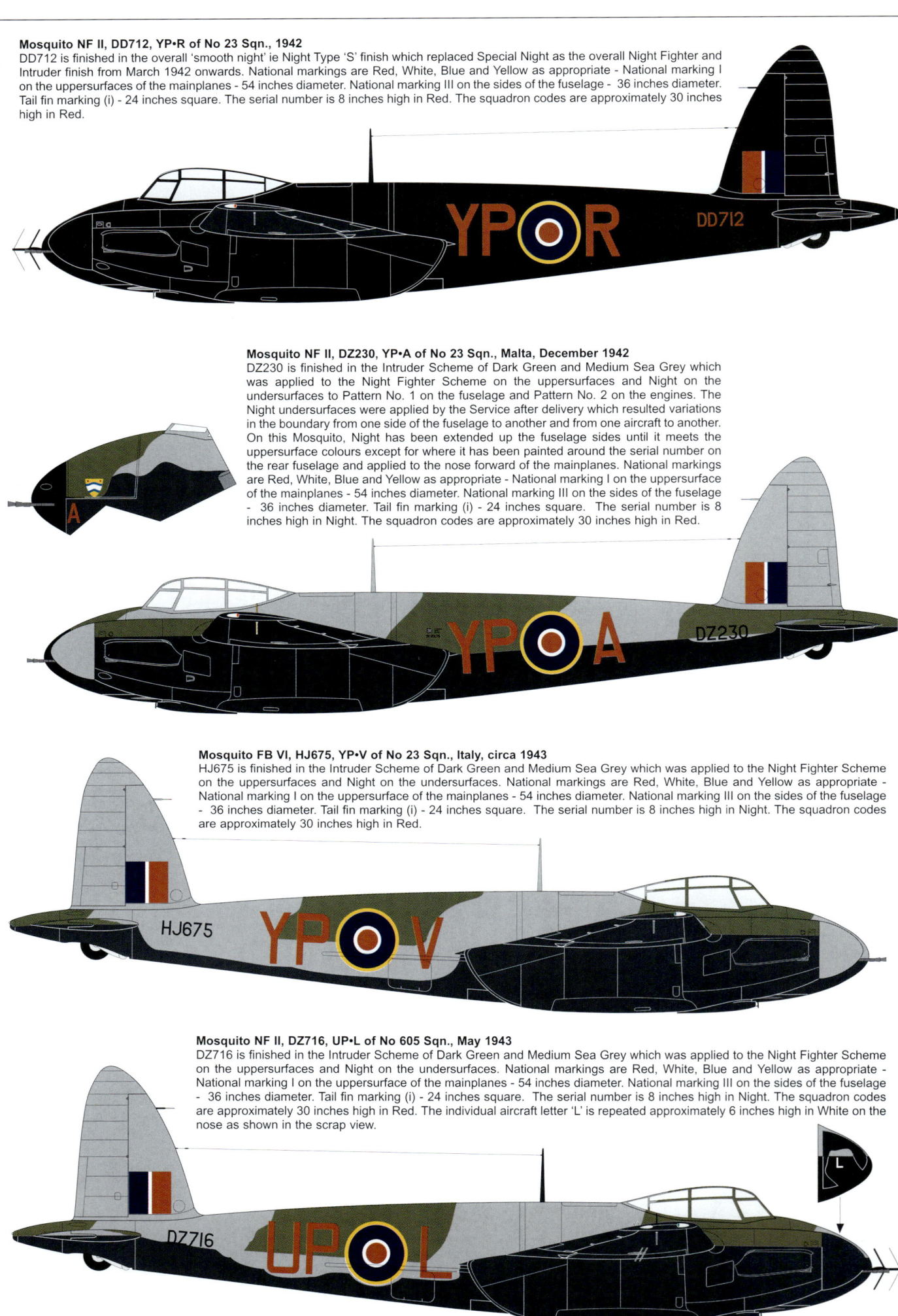

Mosquito NF II, DD712, YP•R of No 23 Sqn., 1942
DD712 is finished in the overall 'smooth night' ie Night Type 'S' finish which replaced Special Night as the overall Night Fighter and Intruder finish from March 1942 onwards. National markings are Red, White, Blue and Yellow as appropriate - National marking I on the uppersurfaces of the mainplanes - 54 inches diameter. National marking III on the sides of the fuselage - 36 inches diameter. Tail fin marking (i) - 24 inches square. The serial number is 8 inches high in Red. The squadron codes are approximately 30 inches high in Red.

Mosquito NF II, DZ230, YP•A of No 23 Sqn., Malta, December 1942
DZ230 is finished in the Intruder Scheme of Dark Green and Medium Sea Grey which was applied to the Night Fighter Scheme on the uppersurfaces and Night on the undersurfaces to Pattern No. 1 on the fuselage and Pattern No. 2 on the engines. The Night undersurfaces were applied by the Service after delivery which resulted variations in the boundary from one side of the fuselage to another and from one aircraft to another. On this Mosquito, Night has been extended up the fuselage sides until it meets the uppersurface colours except for where it has been painted around the serial number on the rear fuselage and applied to the nose forward of the mainplanes. National markings are Red, White, Blue and Yellow as appropriate - National marking I on the uppersurface of the mainplanes - 54 inches diameter. National marking III on the sides of the fuselage - 36 inches diameter. Tail fin marking (i) - 24 inches square. The serial number is 8 inches high in Night. The squadron codes are approximately 30 inches high in Red.

Mosquito FB VI, HJ675, YP•V of No 23 Sqn., Italy, circa 1943
HJ675 is finished in the Intruder Scheme of Dark Green and Medium Sea Grey which was applied to the Night Fighter Scheme on the uppersurfaces and Night on the undersurfaces. National markings are Red, White, Blue and Yellow as appropriate - National marking I on the uppersurface of the mainplanes - 54 inches diameter. National marking III on the sides of the fuselage - 36 inches diameter. Tail fin marking (i) - 24 inches square. The serial number is 8 inches high in Night. The squadron codes are approximately 30 inches high in Red.

Mosquito NF II, DZ716, UP•L of No 605 Sqn., May 1943
DZ716 is finished in the Intruder Scheme of Dark Green and Medium Sea Grey which was applied to the Night Fighter Scheme on the uppersurfaces and Night on the undersurfaces. National markings are Red, White, Blue and Yellow as appropriate - National marking I on the uppersurface of the mainplanes - 54 inches diameter. National marking III on the sides of the fuselage - 36 inches diameter. Tail fin marking (i) - 24 inches square. The serial number is 8 inches high in Night. The squadron codes are approximately 30 inches high in Red. The individual aircraft letter 'L' is repeated approximately 6 inches high in White on the nose as shown in the scrap view.

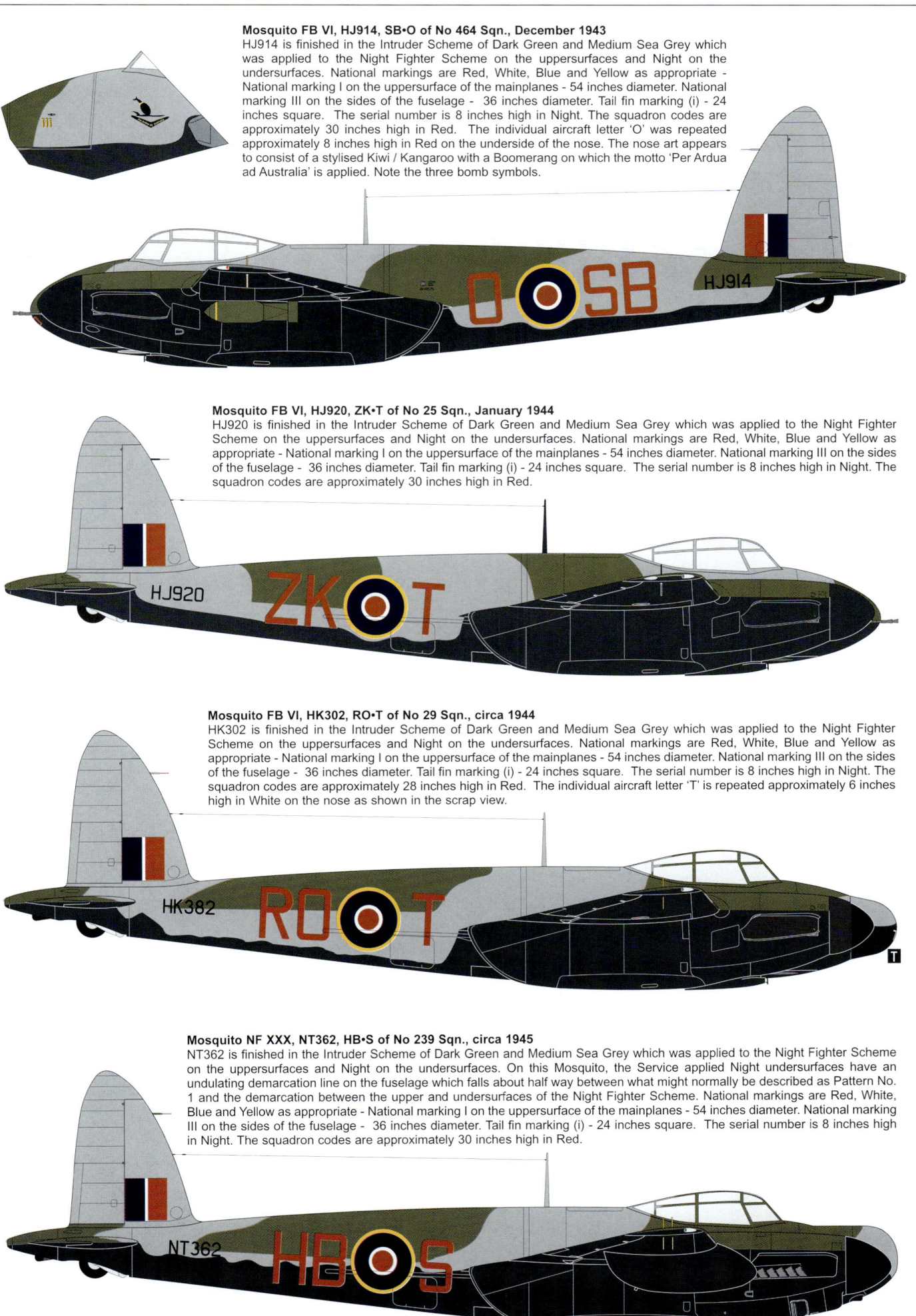

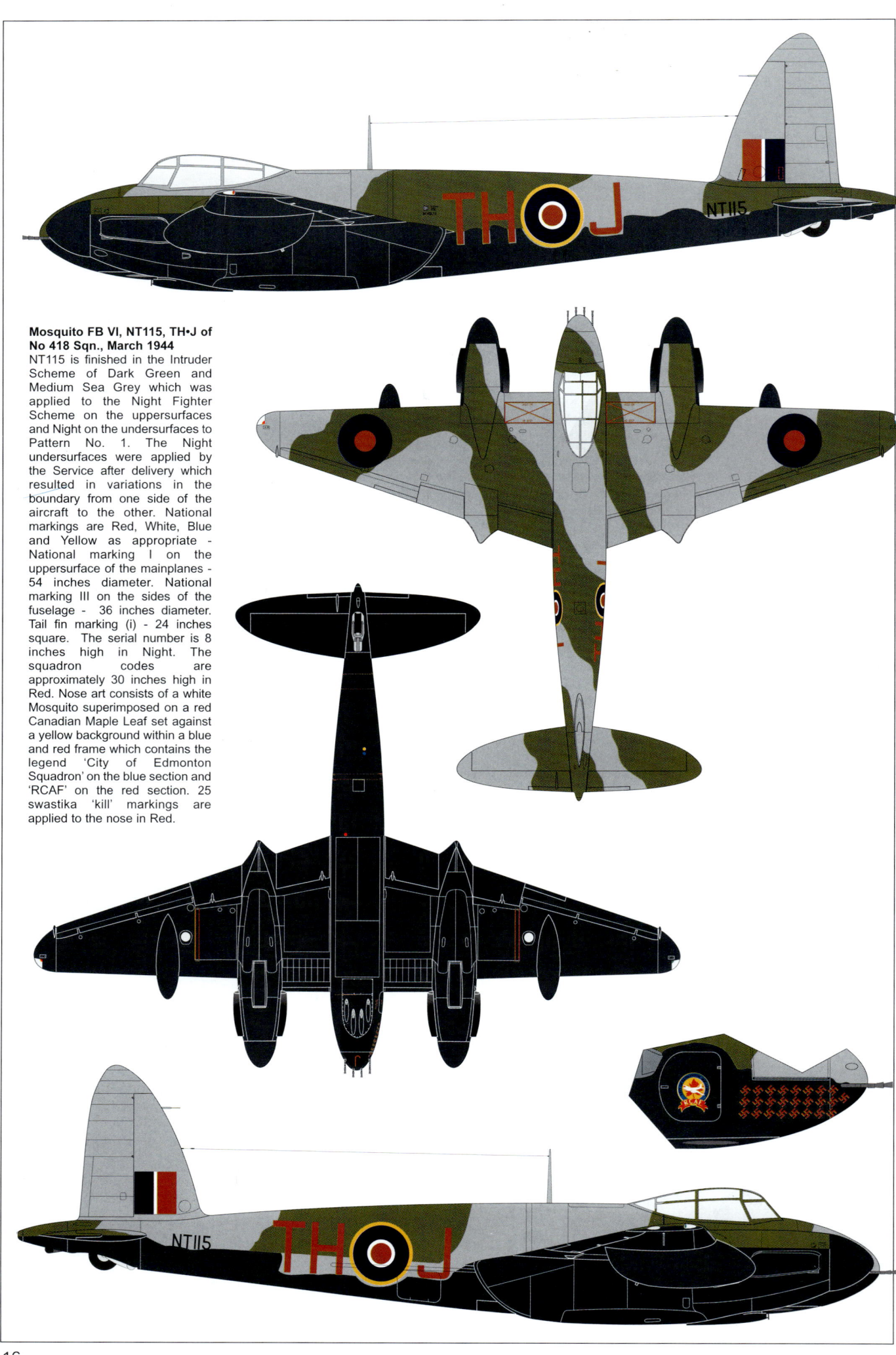

Mosquito FB VI, NT115, TH•J of No 418 Sqn., March 1944

NT115 is finished in the Intruder Scheme of Dark Green and Medium Sea Grey which was applied to the Night Fighter Scheme on the uppersurfaces and Night on the undersurfaces to Pattern No. 1. The Night undersurfaces were applied by the Service after delivery which resulted in variations in the boundary from one side of the aircraft to the other. National markings are Red, White, Blue and Yellow as appropriate - National marking I on the uppersurface of the mainplanes - 54 inches diameter. National marking III on the sides of the fuselage - 36 inches diameter. Tail fin marking (i) - 24 inches square. The serial number is 8 inches high in Night. The squadron codes are approximately 30 inches high in Red. Nose art consists of a white Mosquito superimposed on a red Canadian Maple Leaf set against a yellow background within a blue and red frame which contains the legend 'City of Edmonton Squadron' on the blue section and 'RCAF' on the red section. 25 swastika 'kill' markings are applied to the nose in Red.

Right; Mosquito Mk II (Special), DD712 YP•R of 23 Sqn., September 1942. One of twenty-five Mk IIs specially produced for 23 Sqn without radar and with increased fuel capacity, DD712 is finished in the original Night Fighter/Intruder Scheme of overall Night with the usual national markings and Red serial number. The Red code letters were applied by the Squadron.

the night of 17 September 1942 and actually involved three aircraft:- one finished in Dark Green and Medium Sea Grey; one finished in overall Night; and one camouflaged with Dark Green and Dark Earth on the upper surfaces with Night undersurfaces.

The report on the trial forwarded to HQ Fighter Command from 11 Group on 26 September 1942, stated that the Dark Green and Medium Sea Grey scheme was very easily seen in searchlights both from the ground and in the air, whilst the overall Night scheme was less easily seen in searchlights from the ground. The best camouflage scheme both in or out of searchlights when seen both from the ground and in the air was found to be the Dark Green, Dark Earth and Night camouflaged aircraft, and it was this scheme which was recommended for use on intruder aircraft.

This does not appear to have been well received at Fighter Command who replied to 11 Group on 5 October 1942. 11 Group were informed that it was desirable that the camouflage of Intruder aircraft should coincide as much as possible with the camouflage of ordinary Night Fighter aircraft because the introduction of a variety of colour schemes was extremely upsetting to the manufacturers. It was considered unlikely that the Air Ministry would consent to the introduction of yet another camouflage scheme unless what the letter describes as "......the most cogent reasons exist".

Evidently 11 Group could offer no such reasons as, on 10 October 1942, HQ Fighter Command wrote to the DOR at the Air Ministry setting out the requirements for the camouflage of Intruder aircraft as being Dark Green and Medium Sea Grey on the upper surfaces and Night on the under surfaces. The camouflage on all surfaces was to be as smooth as possible to avoid loss of speed. The final paragraph of this letter asks the Air Ministry to note that this scheme will cause the least possible trouble to manufacturers as it was similar to the scheme adopted for Night Fighters as far as the upper surfaces were concerned with the only change being the application of Night to the under surfaces.

Right: Mosquito Mk II, DD750 was built at Hatfield and delivered between 2 - 12 September 1942, in overall Night with Red serials; (and below) Mosquito Mk II, DZ230, YP•A of 23 Sqn., seen here flying over Malta in 1943, was built at Hatfield and delivered between 13 - 22 October 1942 in the Night Fighter Scheme with Night serials. Taken together, these two photographs would appear to indicate that Hatfield introduced the Night Fighter Scheme of Dark Green and Medium Sea Grey between 12 September and 13 October 1942. The Service applied the Night under surfaces to DZ230 *after* delivery as indicated by the way the demarcation line between the upper and under surfaces goes around the serial number and reveals the original production line demarcation between the upper and under surfaces which can be seen running through the serial number.

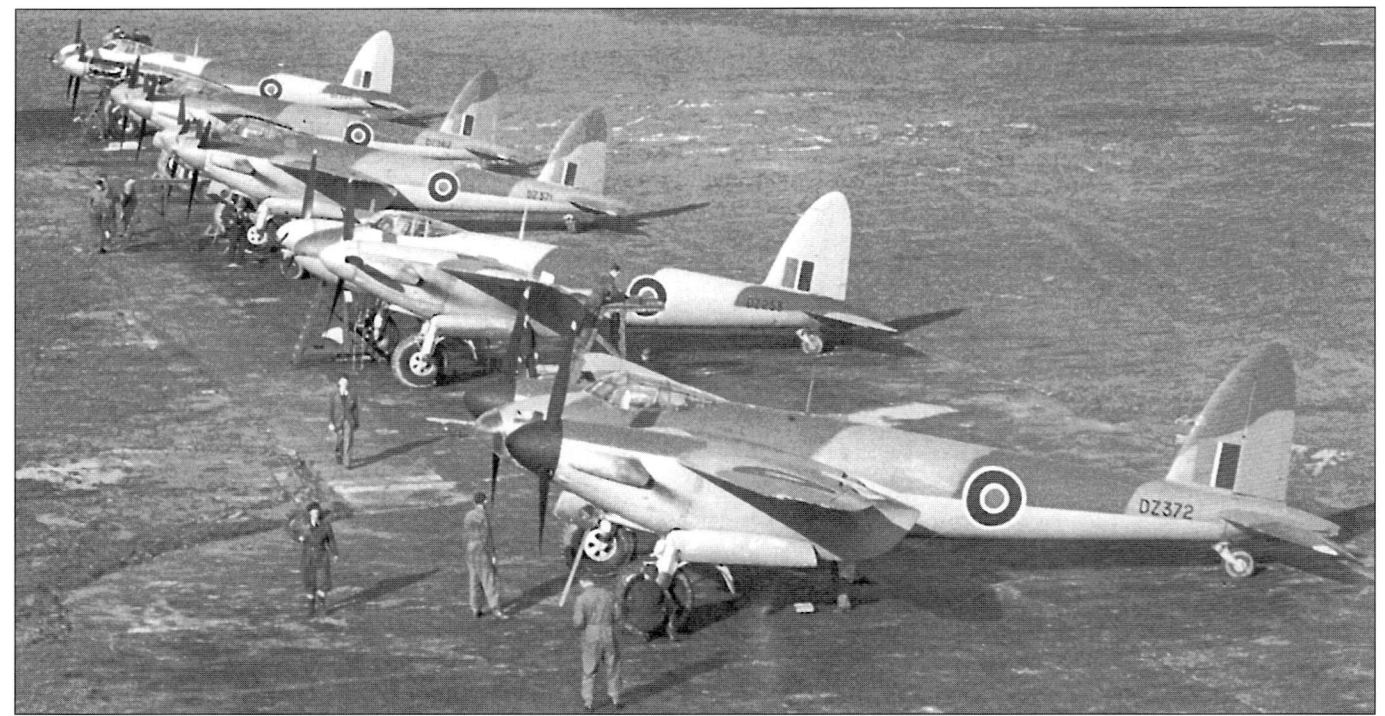

Above Mosquito Mk IIs and IVs at Hatfield in November 1942. This photograph shows to advantage the transposition of colours between Bomber and Fighter Mosquitoes; the Bombers being finished to the 'A' Scheme and the Fighters being finished to the 'C' Scheme. This photo also offers a useful comparison of the relative brightness of both the Day Fighter Scheme seen on the Bombers and the Night Fighter Scheme on the Fighters.

Production changes

How these comparatively rapid changes affected the Mosquito on the production line is not entirely clear; the main problem being the short lived instructions to finish the upper surfaces in the Day Fighter Scheme of Dark Green and Ocean Grey which lasted from (circa) 28 July to (circa) 11 September 1942 - a period of about six weeks.

Some contemporary photographs do however provide us with some information. The photograph of DD750 (on page 17), clearly shows it to have been finished in the overall Night scheme. This Mosquito was delivered between 2 - 12 September. The photograph of DZ230, (also on page 17), delivered between 13 - 22 October shows it to have been finished in the Dark Green and Medium Sea Grey scheme as revealed by the Medium Sea Grey spinners and fin; and the fact that the Night under surfaces, which were applied by 23 Squadron themselves to make the aircraft comply with the Intruder scheme, has been applied around the serial number which has been applied in Night directly on top of the demarcation line between the upper and under surfaces which itself is still visible.

Thus it might be reasonable to suppose that Mosquito NF IIs from DD600 to DD759, were finished in overall Night, whilst the Dark Green and Medium Sea Grey scheme was applied from DZ228 onwards. This leaves a small production batch of NF IIs, (DD777 to DD800), delivered between 21 September and 13 October unaccounted for as they seem to have been rather camera shy prior to delivery. This batch is probably the only batch of NF IIs that might have had the Day Fighter Scheme applied on the production line.

It is of course entirely possible that the Day Fighter Scheme could have been applied to Mosquitoes built earlier, that were either already in service, but if this was the case given the short duration of the scheme's currency, the numbers must have been very small.

When de Havillands began to apply the Night Fighter Scheme of Dark Green and Medium Sea Grey to the Mosquito, they applied the disruptive pattern on the upper surfaces to the pattern shown as Scheme 'A' in Air Diagram 1159 Camouflage Scheme for Twin Engine Monoplanes - Bombers, General Reconnaissance Land Planes, Troop Carriers and Bomber Transports, (all of span less than 75 ft).

When originally published from 1936 onwards, each Air Diagram showed two schemes, one the mirror image of the other. Known as the 'A' and 'B' Schemes, both disruptive patterns were applied to alternate aircraft on the production line until early 1941 when the practice was abandoned as it was thought to be complicating production.

Aircraft manufacturers were then asked to choose one of the two schemes and to apply that scheme to all aircraft in future. De Havillands appear to have chosen the A Scheme for Mosquitoes right from the start of Mosquito production and by late 1942, Mosquito Bombers were being finished in the A Scheme using Dark Green and Ocean Grey.

However, on Mosquitoes finished in the Night Fighter Scheme of Dark Green and Medium Sea Grey, the position of the grey and green segments in the upper surface disruptive pattern was transposed in relation to the Bombers, effectively finishing Mosquito Night Fighters in what might be termed the 'C' Scheme.

Whilst the now well known 'A' and 'B' schemes were illustrated by Air Diagrams drawn up from 1936 onwards, it is of great interest to note that when the RAE was developing the schemes that the Air Diagrams illustrated, they originally had letter/number combinations. Designation L1 was what became the Temperate Land Scheme and in an undated register of Aeroplane camouflage schemes which is believed to be from late 1937, which was preserved in one of the RAE files held by the Public Record Office, the RAE's own designations are set alongside the Air Diagram numbers they became.

Air Diagram 1158 Camouflage Scheme for Single Engine Monoplanes - Medium Bombers was that applied to the Fairey Battle and it has *four* RAE designations: L1A, L1B, L1C, and L1D.

AD 1157 Camouflage Scheme for Twin Engine Monoplanes - Heavy Bombers also has *four* RAE designations: L1F, L1G, L1H, and L1J.

AD 1159 Camouflage Scheme for Twin Engine Monoplanes - Medium Bombers again has *four* RAE designations: L1K, L1L, L1M, and L1N.

Given that two of these designations can be accounted for by the mirror image which became known on the Air Diagrams as the 'A' and 'B' schemes, presumably taken from the RAE designations which were applied to the Fairey Battle diagram which was the first to be drawn up, what is to be made of the two other designations? The most likely explanation is that there were originally intended to be not *two* variants of each colour scheme, (one the mirror image of the other), but *four*. The 'A' and 'B' schemes are well known, so it might be correct to call the other two the 'C' and 'D' schemes. These would most likely have been identical to the 'A' and 'B' schemes, but with the positions of the

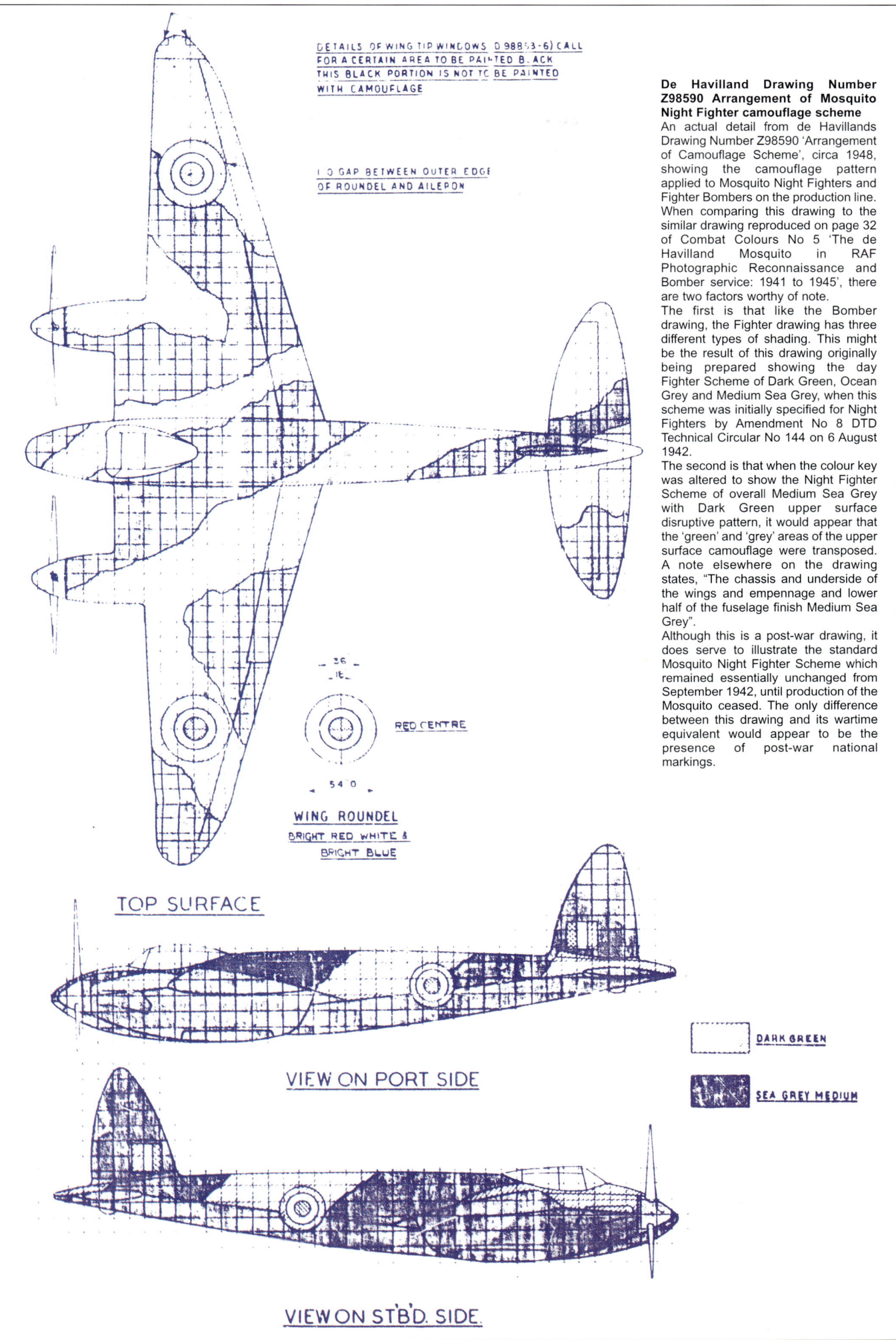

De Havilland Drawing Number Z98590 Arrangement of Mosquito Night Fighter camouflage scheme

An actual detail from de Havillands Drawing Number Z98590 'Arrangement of Camouflage Scheme', circa 1948, showing the camouflage pattern applied to Mosquito Night Fighters and Fighter Bombers on the production line. When comparing this drawing to the similar drawing reproduced on page 32 of Combat Colours No 5 'The de Havilland Mosquito in RAF Photographic Reconnaissance and Bomber service: 1941 to 1945', there are two factors worthy of note.

The first is that like the Bomber drawing, the Fighter drawing has three different types of shading. This might be the result of this drawing originally being prepared showing the day Fighter Scheme of Dark Green, Ocean Grey and Medium Sea Grey, when this scheme was initially specified for Night Fighters by Amendment No 8 DTD Technical Circular No 144 on 6 August 1942.

The second is that when the colour key was altered to show the Night Fighter Scheme of overall Medium Sea Grey with Dark Green upper surface disruptive pattern, it would appear that the 'green' and 'grey' areas of the upper surface camouflage were transposed. A note elsewhere on the drawing states, "The chassis and underside of the wings and empennage and lower half of the fuselage finish Medium Sea Grey".

Although this is a post-war drawing, it does serve to illustrate the standard Mosquito Night Fighter Scheme which remained essentially unchanged from September 1942, until production of the Mosquito ceased. The only difference between this drawing and its wartime equivalent would appear to be the presence of post-war national markings.

Right: Mosquito NF XIII, HK382, RO·T of 29 Sqn circa 1943. HK382 shows the Intruder Scheme to advantage. The upper surfaces are the Dark Green and Medium Sea Grey of the Night fighter Scheme with the original production line demarcation between the upper and under surfaces running approximately half way down the fuselage sides. Following delivery to the Service, Night under surfaces were applied to Pattern No 1 on the fuselage and up the sides of the engine nacelles in the usual Mosquito fashion in order to make the aircraft conform to the Intruder Scheme. Serial numbers are applied in Night and the code letters in Red. Note the significant gap in the demarcation lines between the Dark Green and Night on the fuselage sides. Because the Night under surfaces were applied by the Service, their extent could vary from one aircraft to another. Compare and contrast this photograph with that of DZ230, YP-A of 23 Sqn on the previous page.

Dark Green and Dark Earth transposed.

The transposition of the green and grey segments of the upper surface disruptive camouflage pattern between Mosquito Fighters and Bombers is well illustrated in the photograph reproduced on page 18. The reason why this was done is not known, but this scheme remained unaltered on all subsequent Mosquito Fighter and Fighter Bomber Production.

Such were the speed of the changes to the camouflage of Night Fighters during the period discussed above that the AMOs issued during this period were always behind the existing practice, and it was not until things settled down after September 1942 that they were able to catch up with the issue of AMO A.1377 on 24 December 1942.

Where Mosquitoes were repainted to conform to the new Night Fighter Scheme by the Service, many variations could be seen such as the 'C' Scheme worn by DD739, RX•X of No 456 Sqn., shown previously, finished in accordance with AMOs, and Red serial numbers.

Mosquitoes under pressure

Whilst the Night Fighter Scheme was being sorted out, the Mosquito was forced to take on yet another operational role, that of High Altitude Day Fighter, when August 1942 saw the emergence of a new threat to the security of British airspace in the form of the Junkers Ju 86P.

From 10 August onwards, a small number of these aircraft had mounted a mix of bombing and reconnaissance flights over the UK with near impunity as the RAF's existing fighters could barely reach sufficient altitude to intercept the raiders which were flying at heights of between 38 - 42,000 ft. At that time, the only aircraft in Britain which might be expected to be able to reach those kinds of heights and be able to fight effectively when it got there was a prototype high altitude Mosquito bomber that de Havillands were developing equipped with Merlin 61 engines and a pressure cabin.

Between 7 and 14 September, the prototype Pressure Cabin Bomber, MP469, was modified by fitting a fighter nose with four 0.303 inch Brownings, (taken from DD715 when that aircraft was modified to take centrimetric radar in a 'thimble' radome in the nose), four blade propellers, extended wingtips and smaller diameter wheels as well as other modifications to lighten the structure. A test flight on 14 September showed that MP469 could reach an altitude of 43,500 ft, and on 15 September the aircraft was flown to Northolt to await the enemy.

The photograph of MP469 reproduced on page 22 overleaf is thought to have been taken at de Havillands on or about 14/15 September 1942, and appears to show the converted aircraft to have been finished in a two-tone disruptive camouflage scheme on the upper surfaces and a single quite dark colour on the under surfaces. All the demarcation lines for the three camouflage colours seem to have a very soft edges, quite unlike the comparatively sharp edges on production Mosquitoes.

Because it started life as a prototype bomber, it is thought that MP469 would originally have been finished in Dark Green and Ocean Grey on the upper surfaces and Yellow on its under surfaces. After modification to the high altitude fighter role in September however, the whole aircraft seems to have been repainted as photographs show that the disruptive pattern on the upper surfaces now conforms to that applied to Night Fighters, but with the pattern extended over the fin and rudder. The undersurfaces are a single apparently dark colour whose boundaries on the fuselage are somewhat uncertain whilst those on the engines appear to conform to those of Mosquito Bombers.

At the time of writing there is no hard evidence as to *exactly what* these colours were, but it seems to be generally thought that the upper surface colours are shades of grey and green whilst the under surfaces were blue.

In the author's opinion there at least three plausible interpretations of the available photographic evidence with regard to the upper surface colours, and two with regard to the under surface colours:-

• Dark Green and Ocean Grey
These colours are of course those of the Day Fighter Scheme which by August 1942 was in widespread use with Fighter Command. In addition to this, the aircraft industry was notified of the required change to Dark Green and Ocean Grey upper surfaces for Night Fighters to the pattern shown in Air Diagram 1159 by Amendment No 8 to DTD Technical Circular No 144 on 6 August 1942, so it may not be unreasonable to assume that de Havilland's began to draw up a camouflage scheme for Night Fighter Mosquitoes using these colours in the following weeks, and that this is the scheme which was applied to MP469.

Possible evidence for this is to be seen by the patch of what might be Dark Green on the top of the fin as the later Dark Green and Medium Sea Grey Scheme called for the fin and rudder to be Medium Sea Grey only; de Havilland's probably held stocks of Ocean Grey as it would appear that Ocean Grey was just starting to make its appearance on the Bomber production line at Hatfield at about this same time as the first B IV known to have been finished in the Day Fighter Scheme of Dark Green, Ocean Grey and Medium Sea Grey, DK328, was completed around the middle of August and delivered to 105 Sqn on 29 August 1942.

The biggest problem with this interpretation is that the upper surfaces have apparently been completely repainted. If the upper surface colours were the Dark Green and Ocean Grey of a Mosquito Bomber in the Day Fighter Scheme, why go to the time and trouble of repainting the whole aircraft, transposing the positions of the green and grey in the process when the aircraft was needed as a matter of operational urgency and modifications were for the most part confined to the nose area and wingtips which would have needed minimal touching up to conform to the rest of the camouflage? A second factor is that the shade of grey apparent in the photograph reproduced here appears to be too light to be Ocean Grey. The comparatively pale tone is perhaps more suggestive of Medium Sea Grey.

• Dark Green and Medium Sea Grey
This interpretation supposes that de Havilland's knew of the new Night Fighter Scheme by mid September. However, the camouflage demarcation lines are not

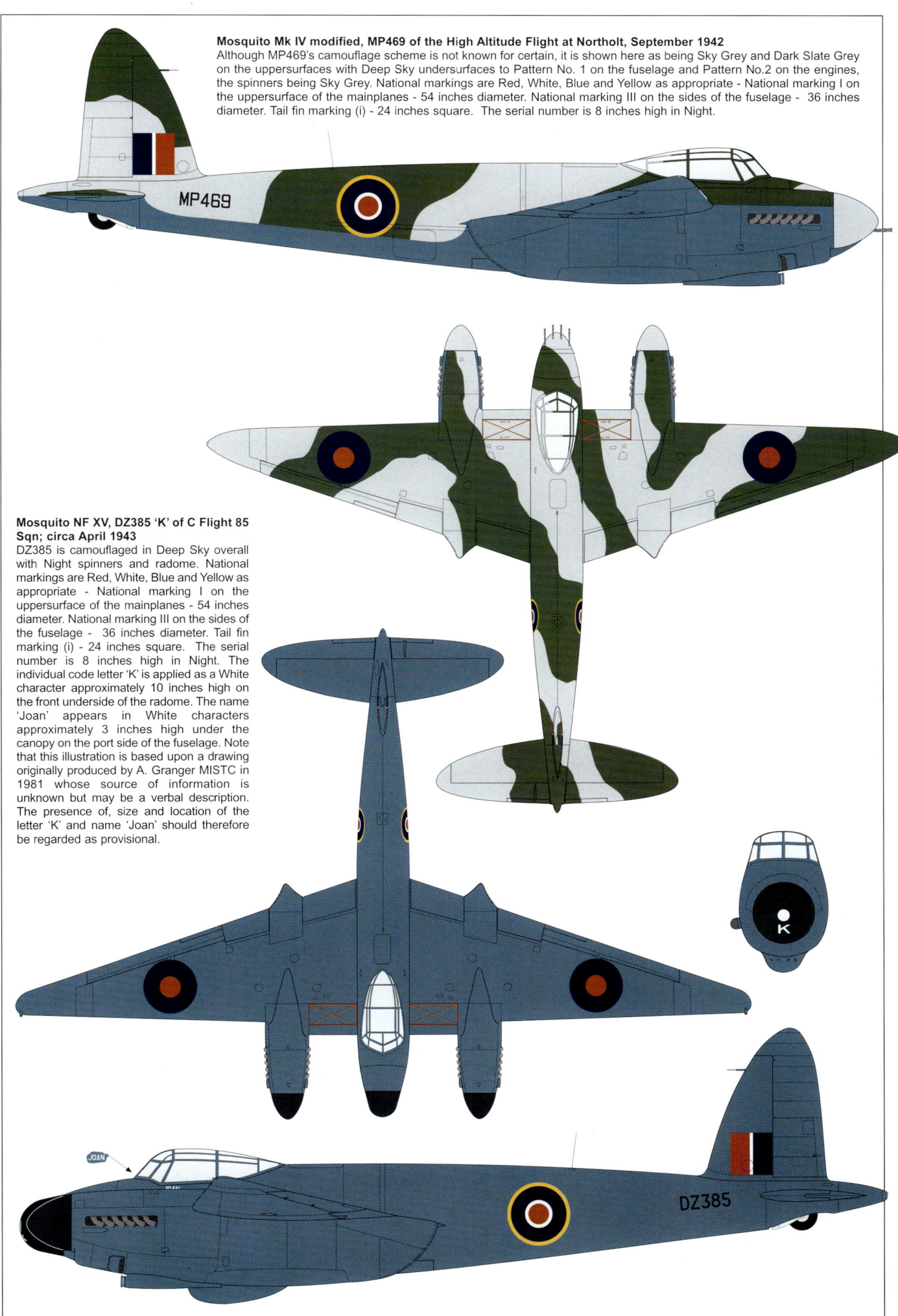

Mosquito Mk IV modified, MP469 of the High Altitude Flight at Northolt, September 1942
Although MP469's camouflage scheme is not known for certain, it is shown here as being Sky Grey and Dark Slate Grey on the uppersurfaces with Deep Sky undersurfaces to Pattern No. 1 on the fuselage and Pattern No.2 on the engines, the spinners being Sky Grey. National markings are Red, White, Blue and Yellow as appropriate - National marking I on the uppersurface of the mainplanes - 54 inches diameter. National marking III on the sides of the fuselage - 36 inches diameter. Tail fin marking (i) - 24 inches square. The serial number is 8 inches high in Night.

Mosquito NF XV, DZ385 'K' of C Flight 85 Sqn; circa April 1943
DZ385 is camouflaged in Deep Sky overall with Night spinners and radome. National markings are Red, White, Blue and Yellow as appropriate - National marking I on the uppersurface of the mainplanes - 54 inches diameter. National marking III on the sides of the fuselage - 36 inches diameter. Tail fin marking (i) - 24 inches square. The serial number is 8 inches high in Night. The individual code letter 'K' is applied as a White character approximately 10 inches high on the front underside of the radome. The name 'Joan' appears in White characters approximately 3 inches high under the canopy on the port side of the fuselage. Note that this illustration is based upon a drawing originally produced by A. Granger MISTC in 1981 whose source of information is unknown but may be a verbal description. The presence of, size and location of the letter 'K' and name 'Joan' should therefore be regarded as provisional.

those of the Night Fighter Scheme as shown by the disruptive pattern on the fin and rudder, and whether de Havilland's had been informed of the new Night Fighter Scheme by the time MP469 was completed on 14 September is open to question.

A letter from the Air Ministry to HQ Fighter Command dated 7 September 1942, mentions that the MAP had been informed of Fighter Command's requirement for the Dark Green and Medium Sea Grey Night Fighter Scheme and the Air Ministry promulgated the new scheme to the Service by Postagram on 11 September. As far as de Havilland's are concerned it is known that NF IIs down to DD750 were being delivered to the RAF during early September 1942 in overall Night, indeed one such Mosquito is parked just behind MP469 in the photograph.

In addition it is possible to use the same argument with regard to the presence of Dark Green in the scheme, ie if Dark Green is present in the scheme, why repaint the whole aircraft, why not just repaint the Ocean Grey areas with Medium Sea Grey?
- Olive Grey or Dark Slate Grey and Medium Sea Grey or Sky Grey

Perhaps the most satisfactory interpretation of the available evidence is that MP469 was finished in a similar manner to Mosquitoes previously camouflaged for operations at high altitude, ie Mosquito PR Is and PR IVs.

The development and use of these colour schemes was covered in some detail in 'Combat Colours No 5'. There was therefore a high altitude camouflage scheme known to de Havillands which might have been considered suitable for application to a high altitude fighter, the application of which would necessitate the repainting of the whole aircraft.

As to which colours were used, it is the author's opinion that one might possibly be Dark Slate Grey, of which de Havilland's might have had remaining supplies following the adoption of an overall PRU Blue finish on PR versions of the Mosquito which is thought to have taken place some time over the summer of 1942.

Unfortunately the identity of the lighter colour is not so clear cut. It is thought that Sky Grey was used on PR IVs due to the difficulty of obtaining adequate supplies of Medium Sea Grey in the early part of 1942 and it is possible that de Havilland's still had a small amount of Sky Grey in stock, but by September 1942, Medium Sea Grey was available at de Havillands in quantity as it was being applied to the undersurfaces of Mosquito B IVs.

The undersurface colour is equally problematic but it would appear that there are only two possibilities - PRU Blue and Deep Sky.

PRU Blue originated as a camouflage colour for Photographic Reconnaissance aircraft in 1940 and was adopted as a standard camouflage colour by the RAF in October 1941. PRU Blue was readily available to de Havillands who were applying it to Photographic Reconnaissance Mosquitoes during the summer of 1942.

Deep Sky had been developed by the RAE for use on high altitude aircraft during 1941 but was apparently little used because the main prospective users, Bomber Command, had been deprived of their supply of Heavy Day Bombers which would have utilised this colour when the United States entered the war in December 1941 and promptly impressed the B-17E and B-24Ds which Bomber Command had expected to take delivery of during 1942.

Deep Sky was a much darker blue than PRU Blue as it had been developed for use at greater altitudes than PRU Blue and it has to be said that the photograph reproduced here suggests that the under surfaces were a very dark colour, this being particularly noticeable on the undercarriage door which catches a great deal of light. De Havillands do not appear to have held stocks of Deep Sky, (as will become apparent when the production of what became known as the Mosquito NF XV is examined later), but as with Olive Grey, it might have been possible for de Havillands to have obtained a small quantity for a specific purpose direct from the RAE.

MP469 appears to have carried National marking I on the uppersurfaces of the wings, National marking III on both sides of the fuselage and Fin marking (i) on the fin with its serial number in Night in the usual place on the rear fuselage. No markings appear to have been applied under the wings and it is not known if any other markings were applied for the short time the aircraft was based at Northolt.

MP469 never met the enemy, as a partially successful interception by a

Above: Mosquito MP469 modified into a high altitude fighter thought to have been photographed at Hatfield circa 14/15 September 1942. The disruptive camouflage scheme on the upper surfaces is thought to have possibly been Sky Grey and Dark Slate Grey whilst the dark tone of the under surfaces may be suggestive of Deep Sky.

Right: Mosquito NF XV DZ385 circa early 1943. DZ385 shows the impressively stretched wings and overall Deep Sky camouflage of the NF XV to advantage. The national markings are all standard size and colour with Night serials. Note the Night radome and spinners. All five Mosquito NF XVs served with C Flight of No 85 Sqn., from March to August 1943.

modified Spitfire IXc on 12 September followed by a spell of bad weather discouraged the Germans from further operations. However, concerns then began to be raised about he possibility of the Junkers being used at night and after MP469 was returned to de Havillands in early October, AI Mk VIII was installed in a thimble nose with the four Brownings being moved to a blister under the fuselage. These modifications were judged successful and it was decided to build another four similar aircraft which were to be designated the NF XV.

Mosquito NF XV

On 11 November 1942, the Resident Technical Officer (RTO) at de Havillands wrote to the RAE at Farnborough requesting a quantity of Deep Sky Type 'S' as it was understood that the RAE would be able to supply this material. The first consignment was to be collected by de Havillands some time over the next few days with a further balance of their requirement from an RAF Maintenance Unit. Thus Deep Sky was applied to the Mosquito NF. XV which began flying in December 1942.

AMO A 1377 issued on 24 December 1942, did not lay down any regulations as to how such aircraft were to be painted. It did however introduce a new heading called 'High altitude fighters' which stated, "Pending the adoption of a standard scheme the various camouflages, colourings and markings used are promulgated to the defences by Postagram or Signal".

This is exactly what happened when the Mosquito NF XV began flying regularly in March 1943. On 8 March, an internal Air Ministry memo raised the possibility of promulgating the colour scheme carried by the Mosquito NF XV and the fact that only a few of this aircraft type had been produced. By 21 March, the first deliveries were taking place to 'C' Flight of 85 Sqn at Hunsdon and on 26 March 1943 the Air Ministry notified all concerned by Postagram that Mosquito Night Fighters normally bore the standard camouflage colouring and marking scheme but some aircraft would be seen coloured Deep Sky on all external surfaces and carrying national markings.

Thus the Mosquito NF XV was finished in Deep Sky overall and carried National marking I on the upper surfaces of the wings; National marking III on both sides of the fuselage; and Fin marking (i) on the fin, with its serial number in Night in the usual place on the rear fuselage. No markings appear to have been applied under the wings. It is not known if squadron codes were carried by the Mosquito XVs of 85 Squadron, it is thought that only the individual aircraft letter was carried on the underside of the radome.

Distinctive markings for 'Operation Overlord'

As part of the planning for the invasion of Europe, 'Operation Overlord', it was decided that Allied aircraft should carry prominent distinctive markings to facilitate the identification of Allied aircraft by friendly land, sea and air forces. When SHAEF Operational Memorandum No 23 which described these markings was first issued in April 1944, Night Fighters were amongst those aircraft not required to wear the distinctive markings. However, within 24 hours of 'Operation Overlord' beginning HQ AEAF found it necessary to send Message A-104, dated 7 June 1944, to Air Defence Great Britain and all its Operational Groups stating that with effect from 8 June all AEAF Night Fighter and Intruder aircraft operating over or near shipping lanes and assault areas during the hours of daylight would carry the distinctive markings as laid down in SHAEF Operational Memorandum.

Twin engined aircraft such as the Mosquito were to be painted on both the upper and under surfaces of their wings from the engine nacelles outwards with five white and black stripes each twenty four inches wide arranged in order from the centre of the aircraft outwards white, black, white, black, white. Fuselages were to be painted with five parallel black and white stripes, each of which were once again to be twenty four inches wide completely around the fuselage with the outside edge of the rearmost band eighteen inches from the leading edge of the tailplane. Appendix A to the memo contained a small drawing showing these markings applied to an outline of a Mosquito.

These markings then remained in place unchanged for a month until, on 6 July 1944, the Allied Expeditionary Air Force (AEAF) recommended that no further aircraft should be given the distinctive markings and that those already applied should be allowed to fade out and not be renewed. Approval for this must have been given promptly, perhaps by telephone as the same day saw HQ AEAF give permission for some aircraft to only carry the distinctive markings on the undersides. This would appear to have been originally intended for the benefit of Air Observation Post aircraft which were proving difficult to conceal on the ground at their forward bases when marked as specified by SHAEF Operational Memorandum 23.

This permission was seen by others as being blanket permission to dispense with the upper surface markings and from 10 July, the American 8th Air Force carried the distinctive markings on the under surfaces only.

As is often the case, it took officialdom a while to catch up with what was happening on the front line squadrons, and it was not until 19 August 1944 that Amendment No 3 to SHAEF Operational Memorandum 23 was issued. This stated that the distinctive black and white marking would be removed from aircraft wings, but that the markings around the fuselage would remain. The period 25 August to 10 September 1944 was allotted for the removal of the markings. It was acknowledged that some units might experience some difficulty in removing these markings from their aircraft, especially on some wood and fabric surfaces without damaging the structure and that as a consequence, the wing markings might still be found on some aircraft after 10 September.

In practice this meant that a wide variety of markings could be seen on Mosquito Night Fighters and Intruders during the late summer and early autumn of 1944 which might range from a full set of distinctive markings to just having them on the underside of the rear fuselage.

Ultimately SHAEF Operational memorandum No 23 was suspended from 31 December 1944 except for the PR aircraft of 34 Wing 2nd TAF which were to retain their markings until such time as notified by 2nd TAF.

As far as is known, no further alterations were officially made in the camouflage and marking of Mosquito Night Fighters and Intruders before the end of the war in Europe.

Left: Mosquito NF XIII, MM571 of 264 Sqn., circa July 1944. MM571 was one of the later NF XIIIs built with the Universal or 'Bull' nose radomes, completed in March 1944. When photographed, MM571 appears to have just joined the Squadron as the area surrounding the code letters appears to have been recently repainted in part over the distinctive under fuselage black and white AEAF 'invasion' stripe markings associated with 'Operation Overlord'. No individual aircraft letter is apparent and the spinners appear to be coloured.

Part Two: Fighter - Bombers

Heading: Mosquito HX917, EG·E of 487 Sqn., circa April 1944. HX917 is finished in the Night Fighter Scheme which was applied to FB VIs on the production line. The national markings were all applied as standard as was the Night serial number. The Sky code letters were applied by the Squadron.

At the time that the meeting to discuss the camouflage requirements of the Mosquito was held at the Air Ministry on 26 January 1942, Mosquito production was seen as being capable of being split into two types from a structural point of view; PRU/Unarmed Bombers and Night Fighter/Fighter Bombers.

The roles within the second structural category were subdivided into Night Fighter, Fighter Bomber, Intruder by Day, Intruder By Night, Escort Fighter and Long Range Fighter. It was thought that the application of different colour schemes to meet specific Command requirements would be impractical from a production point of view, and that the use of different colour schemes with particular markings on the aircraft from different Commands may not be acceptable from a tactical point of view when aircraft from different Commands were operating together.

The suggested solution to this was to apply one colour scheme on the production line to Unarmed Bombers, Fighter Bombers, Long Range Fighters and Escort Fighters. The suggested camouflage scheme for these day flying Mosquitoes was the Temperate Land Scheme of Dark Green and Dark Earth on the upper surfaces and Azure Blue on the under surfaces with the standard national markings as applied to bomber aircraft and squadron codes and individual aircraft letters in Red. The only major variation on this was to be that the Long Range Fighter version for Coastal Command would have its upper surface camouflage changed to the Temperate Sea Scheme of Extra Dark Sea Grey and Dark Slate Grey at the Aircraft Servicing Units prior to issue to squadrons.

At the meeting the view was expressed by the Fighter Command representative that all day flying Mosquitoes should be finished in the Day Fighter Scheme of Dark Green and Ocean Grey upper surfaces with Medium Sea Grey under surfaces as this camouflage scheme had been proved by experience to be an effective compromise for all day conditions. Both Bomber and Coastal Commands ultimately agreed to this proposal.

The markings to be carried on the aircraft were also discussed and the Fighter Command representative put forward the idea that all day flying Mosquitoes should carry the same special recognition markings as were carried by fighter aircraft as a ruse to mislead the enemy. Again both Bomber and Coastal Command ultimately accepted the proposal.

On 6 March 1942 the Air Ministry notified all concerned by Postagram of the camouflage and marking schemes which had been adopted for the Mosquito. This Postagram stated that Mosquitoes with a day role in Fighter, Bomber and Coastal Commands were to bear standard Day Fighter camouflage consisting of Dark Green and Ocean Grey on the upper surfaces with Medium Sea Grey on the under surfaces. Markings were to consist of the serial number applied in the usual way, an 18 inch wide vertical band of Sky around the fuselage immediately forward of the tailplane, Sky spinners and Yellow strips on the leading edges of the wings. Unlike the rest of the markings, for some unknown reason, the Yellow wing leading edge stripes were to be applied by the units when they received the aircraft. The Yellow stripe was to be applied to within 3 feet of the outboard side of the engine nacelle and to be 7 inches wide when measured around the curve of the leading edge tapering to 3 inches wide at the wingtip. The centreline of the stripe was to lie on the centreline of the wing leading edge.

The Ministry of Aircraft Production was thinking along similar lines to the Air Ministry, but perhaps in more detail as on 12 March 1942, an internal MAP memo was circulated discussing the possibility of finishing Fighter-Bomber Mosquitoes in a single colour scheme to aid flexibility in the allotment of these aircraft between separate Commands. It was suggested that if the Mosquitoes were finished on the production line in Medium Sea Grey overall this would provide a suitable base for any day or night camouflage scheme which could then be applied by the ASUs.

This proposal was accepted by the Air Ministry as on 15 March 1942 another Postagram was sent further to the Postagram of 6 March 1942 which informed the recipients that some Mosquito aircraft would be seen flying with all surfaces finished in Medium Sea Grey with Sky spinners and tailbands, standard national markings and the serial number.

All of these instructions appear to have been issued well in advance of any production FB VIs leaving the production lines as on 10 July 1942, the prototype was wrecked at Boscombe Down and a considerable delay then ensued due to production planning decisions with regard to the relative merits of each of the three sub-types - Fighter-Bomber, Intruder and Long Range Fighter - that it was now planned to produce.

When the first production Mosquito FB VIs did emerge in February 1943, they were built on the same production line as the Night Fighter versions and were finished in the Night Fighter Scheme of Dark Green and Medium Sea Grey.

Exactly why this came about is unclear because none of the surviving documents seen by the author at the time of writing throw any light on the subject. Perhaps the most plausible explanation is that when the Night Fighter Scheme was introduced on to the

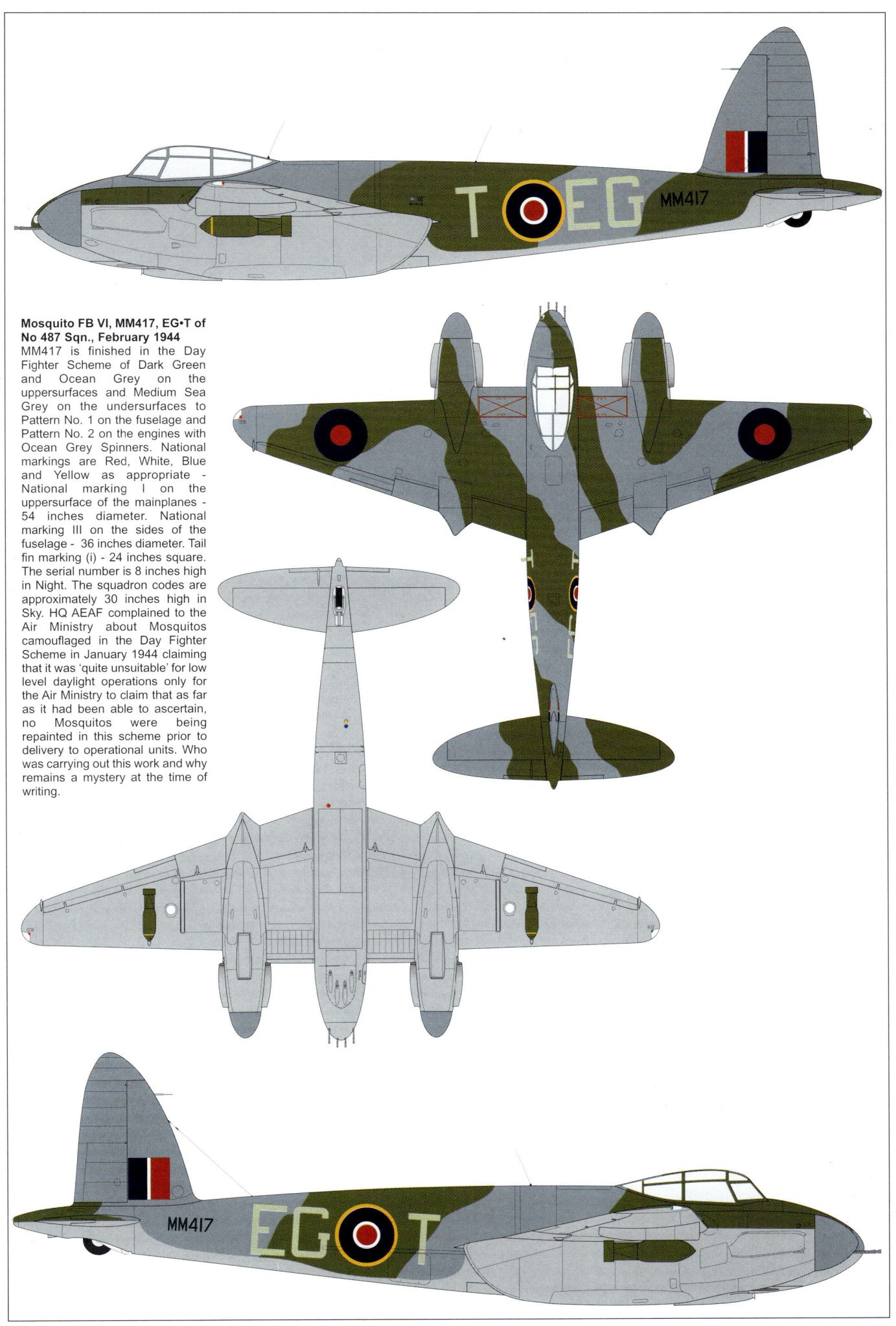

Mosquito FB VI, MM417, EG·T of No 487 Sqn., February 1944

MM417 is finished in the Day Fighter Scheme of Dark Green and Ocean Grey on the uppersurfaces and Medium Sea Grey on the undersurfaces to Pattern No. 1 on the fuselage and Pattern No. 2 on the engines with Ocean Grey Spinners. National markings are Red, White, Blue and Yellow as appropriate - National marking I on the uppersurface of the mainplanes - 54 inches diameter. National marking III on the sides of the fuselage - 36 inches diameter. Tail fin marking (i) - 24 inches square. The serial number is 8 inches high in Night. The squadron codes are approximately 30 inches high in Sky. HQ AEAF complained to the Air Ministry about Mosquitos camouflaged in the Day Fighter Scheme in January 1944 claiming that it was 'quite unsuitable' for low level daylight operations only for the Air Ministry to claim that as far as it had been able to ascertain, no Mosquitos were being repainted in this scheme prior to delivery to operational units. Who was carrying out this work and why remains a mystery at the time of writing.

Right: Mosquito FB VI, MM417, EG·T of 487 Sqn., circa February 1944. This well known photograph shows MM417 to have been finished in the Day Fighter Scheme of Dark Green and Ocean Grey on the upper surfaces to Pattern No 1 by some unknown Service unit. This finish was unpopular with 2 Group who complained to the Air Ministry about Mosquitoes finished in this scheme.

production line, someone in either the Air Ministry and or Ministry of Aircraft Production realised that if Dark Green and Medium Sea Grey were applied on the production line, then it would only require the ASUs to add Ocean Grey to the scheme to convert it to the full Day Fighter Scheme, or Night to convert it to the Intruder Scheme, if required. This would only have been a slight extension of the previously approved idea to finish Mosquitoes in Medium Sea Grey overall.

Some Mosquitoes were definitely finished in the Day Fighter Scheme, although not apparently by the manufacturers. Exactly who was responsible for refinishing the aircraft in the Day Fighter Scheme, and why it was done is unknown. A clue as to why it was done may perhaps be found in Air Ministry Orders A.664/42 and A.1096/42. AMO A.664/42 issued on 2 July 1942, stated that Mosquito aircraft with a day role were to be finished in standard Day Fighter camouflage colouring and markings including Yellow stripes on the leading edges of the wings. These provisions remained in force until amended by AMO A.1096 dated 8 October 1942, which stated that Mosquito aircraft with a day role were to bear standard Day Fighter camouflage and colouring. National and tactical markings were to conform to the scheme for Day Bomber aircraft with Ocean Grey spinners and Sky codes but no other tactical markings.

All these instructions were aimed at Mosquito B IVs because these were the only operational day flying Mosquitoes at the time. With the appearance of day flying FB VIs early in 1943, it would perhaps not be unreasonable for some Service units such as Maintenance Units to view these as day flying Mosquitoes under the terms of AMO A.1096 or even AMO A.664/42 and to treat them accordingly. Photographs certainly show Mosquito FB VIs in the Day Fighter Scheme, some even having Sky tailbands and spinners, possibly as a result of the Postagram of 6 March 1942.

Whoever was responsible for, and the exact reason why, the Day Fighter Scheme was applied is not clear; but what is certain is that the application of the Day Fighter Scheme to Mosquito FB VIs was not popular at Allied Expeditionary Air Force Headquarters.

HQ AEAF wrote to the Air Ministry on 2 January 1944 to complain that Mosquito aircraft being supplied to 2 Group were being delivered in two camouflage schemes, one for Day Fighters and the other for Night Fighters. Of the two, HQ AEAF felt that the Night Fighter Scheme, although not ideal for low-level daylight operations did provide a reasonable compromise for both day and night operations. The Day Fighter camouflage however was darker in tone and considered quite unsuitable for low-level daylight operations for which a lighter scheme was felt necessary to protect aircraft from visual detection at a distance.

The letter then went on to inform the Air Ministry that experiments had been carried out with the collaboration of the RAE at Farnborough with a view to devising a new camouflage scheme which was not only completely suitable for low-level daylight operations but would also afford a reasonable degree of protection during night operations.

This new scheme, which 2 Group wished to adopt consisted of a disruptive pattern of what the letter describes as 'light brown and green' on the upper surfaces with 'night fighter light grey' on the under surfaces, 'light grey' on the spinners, and a 'very light grey or off white' on the fin and rudder.

It was appreciated that this scheme could not be introduced for the benefit of one single Group, but suggested that the adoption of the new scheme for Fighter-Bomber Mosquitoes might be an advantage. As an immediate measure whilst the Air Ministry was considering this proposal, it was requested that all replacement aircraft delivered to 2 Group would be delivered in the Night Fighter Scheme.

The Air Ministry appears to have considered this proposal for about two weeks before replying on 18 January. This reply stated that Mosquito FB VI aircraft were camouflaged in accordance with DTD Technical Circular 360 and should therefore be being delivered in the Night Fighter Scheme. Having looked in to the matter, HQ 41 Group Maintenance Command had informed the Air Ministry that in no instance were Mosquito Fighter-Bombers being re-coloured prior to delivery to operational units and that detailed information regarding which particular Mosquito aircraft had been received in the Day Fighter Scheme was required so that the source where this camouflage was

Right: Mosquito FB VI, LR275, SY·B of 613 Sqn., circa January 1944. LR275 is finished in some interesting camouflage and markings. The upper surfaces are clearly finished in a two colour disruptive scheme to Pattern No 1. The question is whether this is the Day Fighter Scheme of Dark Green and Ocean Grey or an experimental green and brown scheme which is known to have been tried by 2 Group in conjunction with the RAE at about this time. One possible clue is the colour of the fin and rudder which appear to be in a light grey of some kind. A light grey fin was a feature of the experimental scheme whereas Mosquitoes camouflaged in the Day Fighter Scheme seem to have had their fins finished in one or other of the upper surface colours. On the other hand, the Sky spinners and tailband were sometimes a feature of Mosquitoes finished in the Day Fighter Scheme.

applied could be traced and remedial action taken.

Unfortunately no document seen by the author at the time of writing throws any light on this matter and the question of where and why Mosquitoes were being finished in this manner remains open to question.

With regard to the request for the new camouflage scheme to be applied to Mosquito FB VIs, the Air Ministry stated that Mosquito Fighter-Bomber and Night Fighter aircraft were built on the same production lines and that it was impractical to differentiate between these roles for the purpose of applying distinctive colour schemes and that the introduction of a new camouflage scheme for the Mosquito on the production line was therefore not possible.

It was considered undesirable to change the camouflage scheme after production as it was felt that this would incur an adverse effect on the performance of an aircraft, especially the Mosquito, in view of its wooden form of construction. Another factor was the shortage of labour to do the work. It was therefore impossible to give permission for 2 Group to adopt the new colour scheme.

Unfortunately no record appears to have survived giving precise details of what this camouflage scheme might have looked like. The upper surface colours, 'light brown and green' can be interpreted in several different ways. Did they mean light brown and light green or light brown and a dark green? Light brown could mean Light Earth, or Dark Earth viewed in strong sunshine. Night Fighter light grey is almost certainly Medium Sea Grey whilst very light grey and off white are open to any interpretation.

Intriguingly, the photograph of LR275, SY•B of No 613 Sqn., at Lasham shows what appears to be a two-tone disruptive camouflage pattern on the upper surfaces with a Sky tailband and spinners - and the fin and rudder appear to be a single shade of light grey! It is perhaps most likely that the upper surface colours were Dark Green and Ocean Grey, but if this is the case, then LR275 would have been unusual in retaining a Medium Sea Grey fin and rudder as all the other photographs seen by the author of Mosquitoes finished in the Day Fighter Scheme show the fin and rudder to have also been finished in the upper surface colours.

Given that it is known that 2 Group were experimenting with a form of camouflage which involved finishing Mosquitoes with a light grey fin and rudder and that Ocean Grey reflected 16 percent of diffuse light whilst Dark Earth reflected 13 percent which makes the two colours impossible to tell apart in black and white photographs, it is possible that LR275 carried a 'green, brown and grey scheme'. The colour artwork showing LR275 in such a scheme which is presented here should be regarded as highly provisional until such time as evidence to either confirm or refute it comes to light.

The provisions of AMO A.1096/42 remained in force until the issue of AMO A.864/44 on 7 September 1944, which stated that camouflage and markings were set out in DTD Technical Circular No 360. The following month this tech circular formed the basis for part of Air Publication 2656A Internal and External Finish of Aircraft.

AP 2656A proved to be equally as vague as to the camouflage and markings of Mosquito Fighter-Bombers as all that had gone before. Whilst Mosquito Day Bombers in the Day Fighter Scheme are specifically mentioned, no mention is made of Fighter-Bombers, and as far as is known, the Night fighter Scheme continued to be applied to all FB VIs on the production lines until production ceased.

'Operation Overlord' markings

Whilst no alteration in Mosquito camouflage took place during early 1944, it will be recalled that SHAEF Operational Memorandum No 23 first began to be circulated in April 1944. The stated object of this memorandum was to describe the distinctive markings to be applied to aircraft of the United States and Britain for 'Operation Overlord' in order to make them more easily identified as friendly by ground and naval forces as well as by other friendly aircraft.

Fighter-Bomber aircraft were amongst those aircraft specifically cited in the paragraph which dealt with the scope of the memo which was to become effective on the day of the assault and thereafter until it was deemed advisable to change.

As the character and chronology of these markings application to Mosquitoes has already been described in the previous chapter, there in no need to repeat the information here. It should be remembered however that a wide variety of markings could be seen on Mosquitoes during the late summer and early autumn of 1944 which might range from a full set of distinctive markings to just having them on the underside of the rear fuselage.

National marking changes

The Air Ministry was certainly concerned by the number of incidents of mis-identification which were taking place, and it was in an attempt to do something about this that it was decided to revert to a Red, White, and Blue roundel on the upper wing surfaces. Accordingly Cypher AX 110 dated 2 January 1945, from the Air Ministry to all RAF Command Headquarters at home and overseas, Air Staff SHAEF, Headquarters 2nd TAF et al gave notice that with effect from 7th January all aircraft other than those whose primary role was night operations, and aircraft operating in Air Command South East Asia and the Pacific were to revert to red, white, and blue roundels on the upper surfaces of the main planes in place of the Red and Blue National marking I.

Because of the need to replace a large number of different sized National marking Is with the new national marking, no comprehensive list of measurements was given. Instead the size of the roundel was given in fractions of R where R was the radius of the upper wing roundel specified for any particular type of aircraft. The overall diameter of the new roundels Blue segment was to be the same as the roundel it replaced with a White segment half the overall diameter of the roundel, and a Red segment 3/8 the overall diameter of the roundel.

These proportions were in fact the same as those of the National marking II roundel which was applied to the undersurfaces of wings. However, apparently because DTD Technical Circular No. 360 and A.P.2656A specified only three fixed sizes for National marking II, and the new roundel was required in a much larger number of different sizes to suit many different types of aircraft, the new red white and blue roundel was given the official designation 'National marking IA'.

However, 2 TAF had its own ideas on what measures were necessary to ensure the correct identification of its aircraft. On 3 January 1945, HQ 2 TAF sent Signal AO 373 to the Air Ministry stating that present operations had established the need for a clearer means of recognising aircraft. As a consequence 2 TAF was removing the Sky markings on

Left: Mosquito FB VI, MM403, SB•V of 464 Sqn., circa autumn 1944. MM403 is finished in the Day Fighter Scheme with a Sky tailband and codes. Note that this Mosquito appears to have only carried the black and white distinctive markings under the rear fuselage, where it obscures part of the codes, and under the mainplanes.

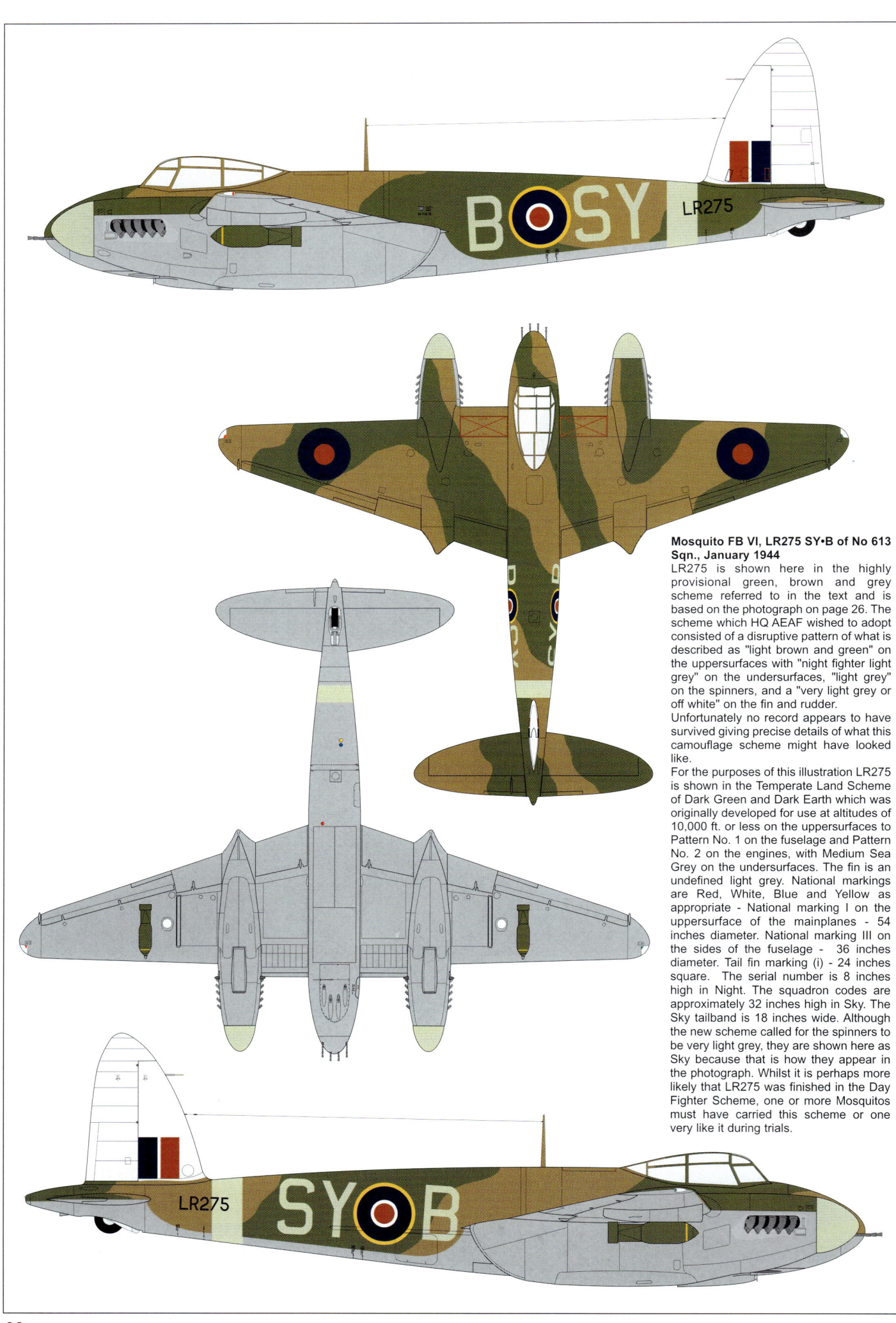

Mosquito FB VI, LR275 SY•B of No 613 Sqn., January 1944

LR275 is shown here in the highly provisional green, brown and grey scheme referred to in the text and is based on the photograph on page 26. The scheme which HQ AEAF wished to adopt consisted of a disruptive pattern of what is described as "light brown and green" on the uppersurfaces with "night fighter light grey" on the undersurfaces, "light grey" on the spinners, and a "very light grey or off white" on the fin and rudder.

Unfortunately no record appears to have survived giving precise details of what this camouflage scheme might have looked like.

For the purposes of this illustration LR275 is shown in the Temperate Land Scheme of Dark Green and Dark Earth which was originally developed for use at altitudes of 10,000 ft. or less on the uppersurfaces to Pattern No. 1 on the fuselage and Pattern No. 2 on the engines, with Medium Sea Grey on the undersurfaces. The fin is an undefined light grey. National markings are Red, White, Blue and Yellow as appropriate - National marking I on the uppersurface of the mainplanes - 54 inches diameter. National marking III on the sides of the fuselage - 36 inches diameter. Tail fin marking (i) - 24 inches square. The serial number is 8 inches high in Night. The squadron codes are approximately 32 inches high in Sky. The Sky tailband is 18 inches wide. Although the new scheme called for the spinners to be very light grey, they are shown here as Sky because that is how they appear in the photograph. Whilst it is perhaps more likely that LR275 was finished in the Day Fighter Scheme, one or more Mosquitos must have carried this scheme or one very like it during trials.

Mosquito FB VI, HX921, SB•H of No 464 Sqn., December 1943
HX921 is finished in the Night Fighter Scheme of Dark Green and Medium Sea Grey on the uppersurfaces and Medium Sea Grey on the undersurfaces. National markings are Red, White, Blue and Yellow as appropriate - National marking I on the uppersurfaces of the mainplane - 54 inches diameter. National marking III on the sides of the fuselage - 36 inches diameter. Tail fin marking (i) - 24 inches square. The serial number is 8 inches high in Night. The squadron codes are approximately 36 inches high in Sky. The spinners are Red. Note the Wing Commanders pennant under the cockpit on the port side of the fuselage.

Mosquito FB VI, HX922, EG•F of No 487 Sqn., February 1944
HX922 is finished in the Night Fighter Scheme of Dark Green and Medium Sea Grey on the uppersurfaces and Medium Sea Grey on the undersurfaces. National markings are Red, White, Blue and Yellow as appropriate - National marking I on the uppersurfaces of the mainplane - 54 inches diameter. National marking III on the sides of the fuselage - 36 inches diameter. Tail fin marking (i) - 24 inches square. The serial number is 8 inches high in Night. The squadron codes are approximately 30 inches high in Sky. This is the Mosquito in which Group Captain P.C. Pickard and Flight Lieutenant J.A. Broadley were killed leading the attack on Amiens prison which took place on 18 February 1944 when HX922 was shot down by Fw 190s.

Mosquito FB VI, LR262, SM•Q of No 305 Sqn., 1944
LR262 is finished in the Night Fighter Scheme of Dark Green and Medium Sea Grey on the uppersurfaces and Medium Sea Grey on the undersurfaces. National markings are Red, White, Blue and Yellow as appropriate - National marking I on the uppersurfaces of the mainplane - 54 inches diameter. National marking III on the sides of the fuselage - 36 inches diameter. Tail fin marking (i) - 24 inches square. The serial number is 8 inches high in Night. The squadron codes are approximately 33 inches high in Sky. Note the Red and White Polish badge on the nose as shown in the scrap view.

Mosquito FB VI, LR366, SY•L of No 613 Sqn., spring 1944
LR366 is finished in the Night Fighter Scheme of Dark Green and Medium Sea Grey on the uppersurfaces and Medium Sea Grey on the undersurfaces. National markings are Red, White, Blue and Yellow as appropriate - National marking I on the uppersurfaces of the mainplane - 54 inches diameter. National marking III on the sides of the fuselage - 36 inches diameter. Tail fin marking (i) - 24 inches square. The serial number is 8 inches high in Night. The squadron codes are approximately 28 inches high in Sky.

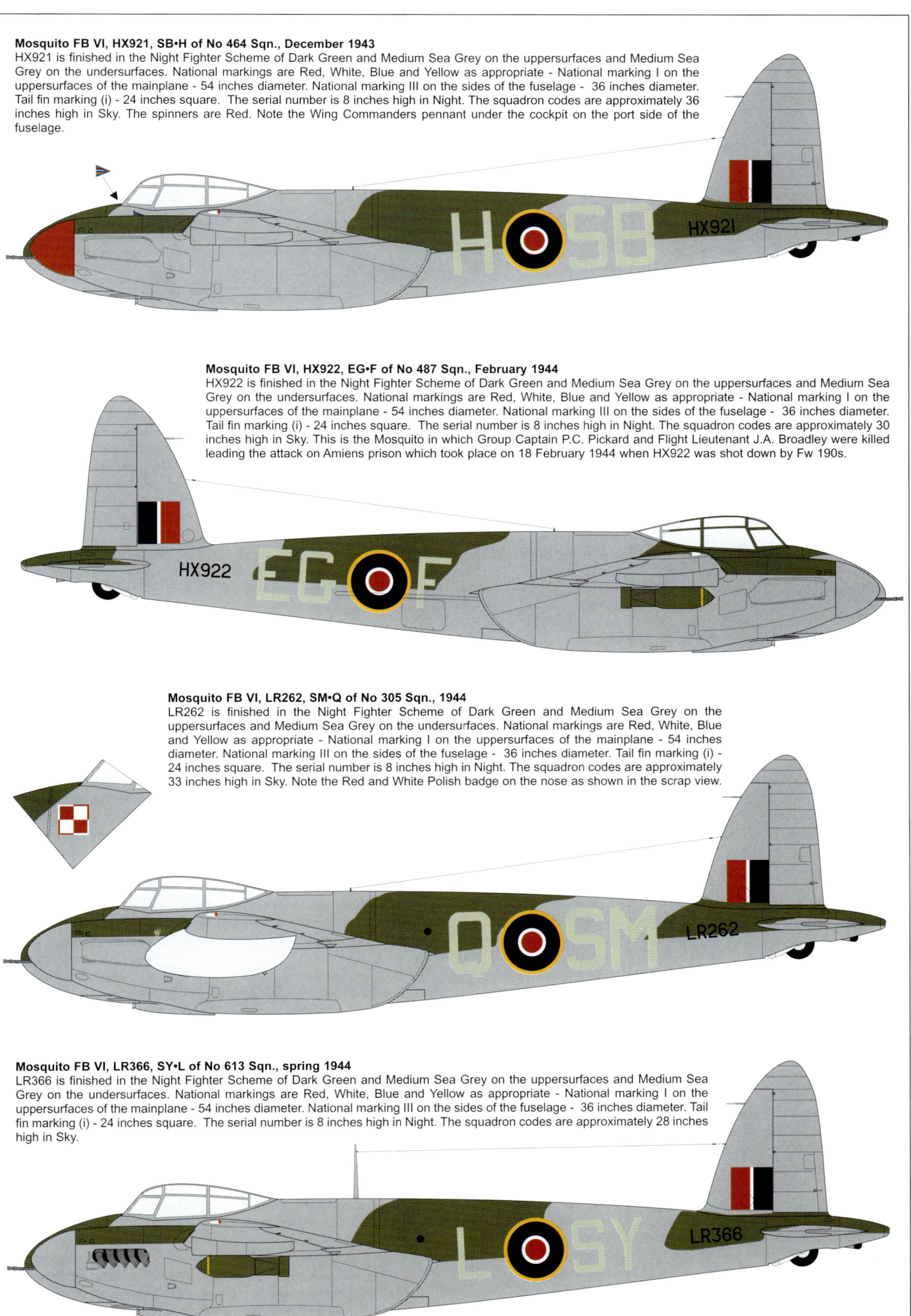

Above: Mosquito FB VI, NT144 SB·A of 464 Sqn., circa early 1945. NT144 is finished in the standard Night Fighter Scheme with the addition of the Red, White, Blue and Yellow National marking III on the upper surfaces of the mainplane as well as on the fuselage. This scheme was typical of 2 TAF Mosquitoes for the remainder of the war.

the spinner and around the rear fuselage on fighter aircraft. Additionally, all roundels on day flying aircraft were to be applied using Red, White, Blue and Yellow in accordance with National marking III of DTD Technical Circular No. 360 Issue 2 and AP 2656A. 2nd TAF requested that the Air Ministry and SHAEF should inform all concerned and that the Air Ministry should arrange for all future deliveries of day flying aircraft to conform with the new requirements.

Whilst the decision to remove the Sky recognition markings from the spinner and around the rear fuselage did not appear to upset the Air Ministry at all, the alterations to the National markings was quite a different matter. On 4 January 1945 the Air Ministry signalled 2 TAF pointing out that Signal AO 373 of 3 January conflicted with the Air Ministry instructions to apply Red, White and Blue roundels to the upper surfaces of the wings of day flying aircraft which had been sent out on 2 January for just this reason. The Air Ministry requested that 2 TAF amend its instructions to conform with those of the Air Ministry while stating that if these alterations in the markings were thought to be really necessary, then the case for them should be submitted for consideration.

HQ 2 TAF submitted its case for the alterations in writing in a letter dated 22 January 1945. The letter stated that the number of instances where Allied aircraft were being shot down by either Allied aircraft or guns due to mistaken identity was causing grave concern. The request was therefore made that the Red, White, Blue, and Yellow National marking

Right: Mosquito FB VI, PZ306, YH·Y of 21 Sqn., circa March 1945. Finished in the Night Fighter Scheme of Dark Green and Medium Sea Grey with Sky codes, PZ306 shows the Red, White, Blue and Yellow National marking IIIs applied to the upper surfaces of the wings of 2 TAF's aircraft from January 1945 onwards to good effect.

should be accepted as standard for all roundel positions on day flying aircraft of that Command.

The Yellow outer band was thought to add to the contrast of the colours on camouflaged aircraft, making the roundels more easily seen and recognised whilst being a very simple means of assisting recognition. Finally, the letter informed the Air Ministry that as no instruction had been received specifically ordering the removal of the Yellow outer bands, it had been decided to continue applying them.

When the Air Ministry failed to take any further action with regard to the application of National marking III the work evidently carried on, as on 5 February, HQ 2 TAF signalled the Air Ministry to inform them that the repainting of the roundels to this type had now been completed. Even so, the matter was far from closed as the Air Ministry was considering the position. It would appear that the Air Ministry's opposition to the change was due to the possibility of confusion by aircraft of other Commands flying over the Continent. A Minute dated 24 March made the point that in the face of 2 TAF's continuing disobedience in the matter, there were two choices open to the Air Ministry. Either 2 TAF's request could be denied again, or all Commands could be signalled to ask if there were any cases of mistaken identity due to the Yellow outer surround to the roundels. In the event of negative replies, the Air Ministry should concede the point to 2 TAF.

It would appear that ultimately the point was conceded and the National marking III's were allowed to remain. They are visible in many of the photographs taken of 2 TAF Mosquitos during the remainder of the European war.

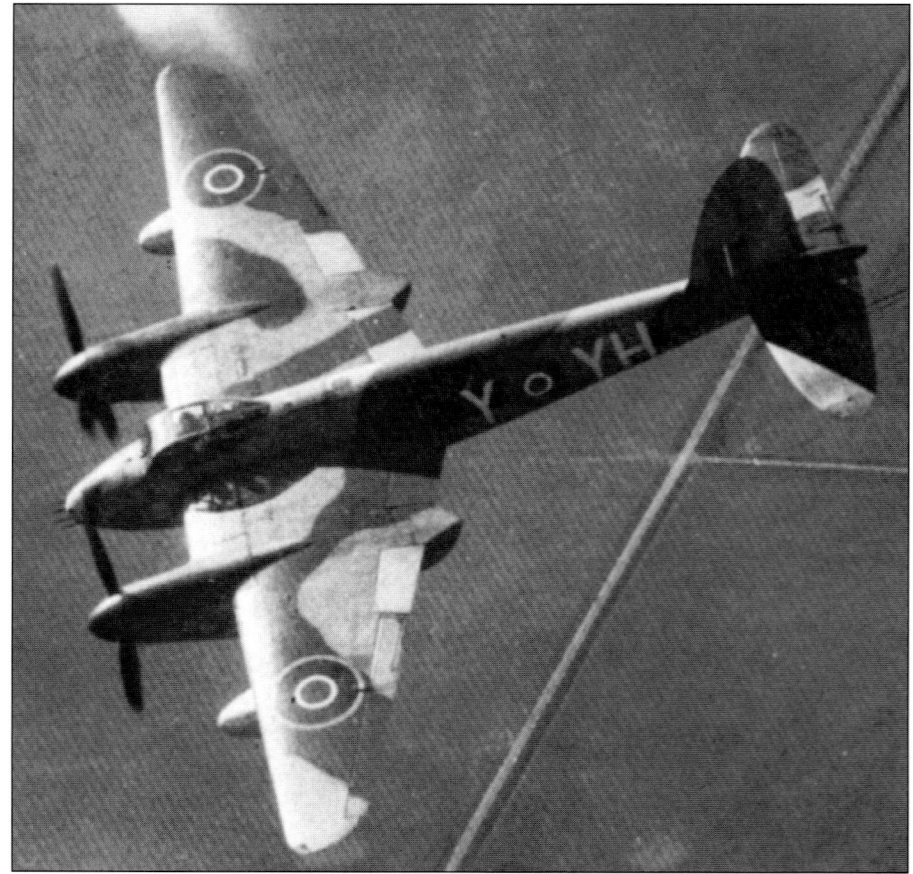

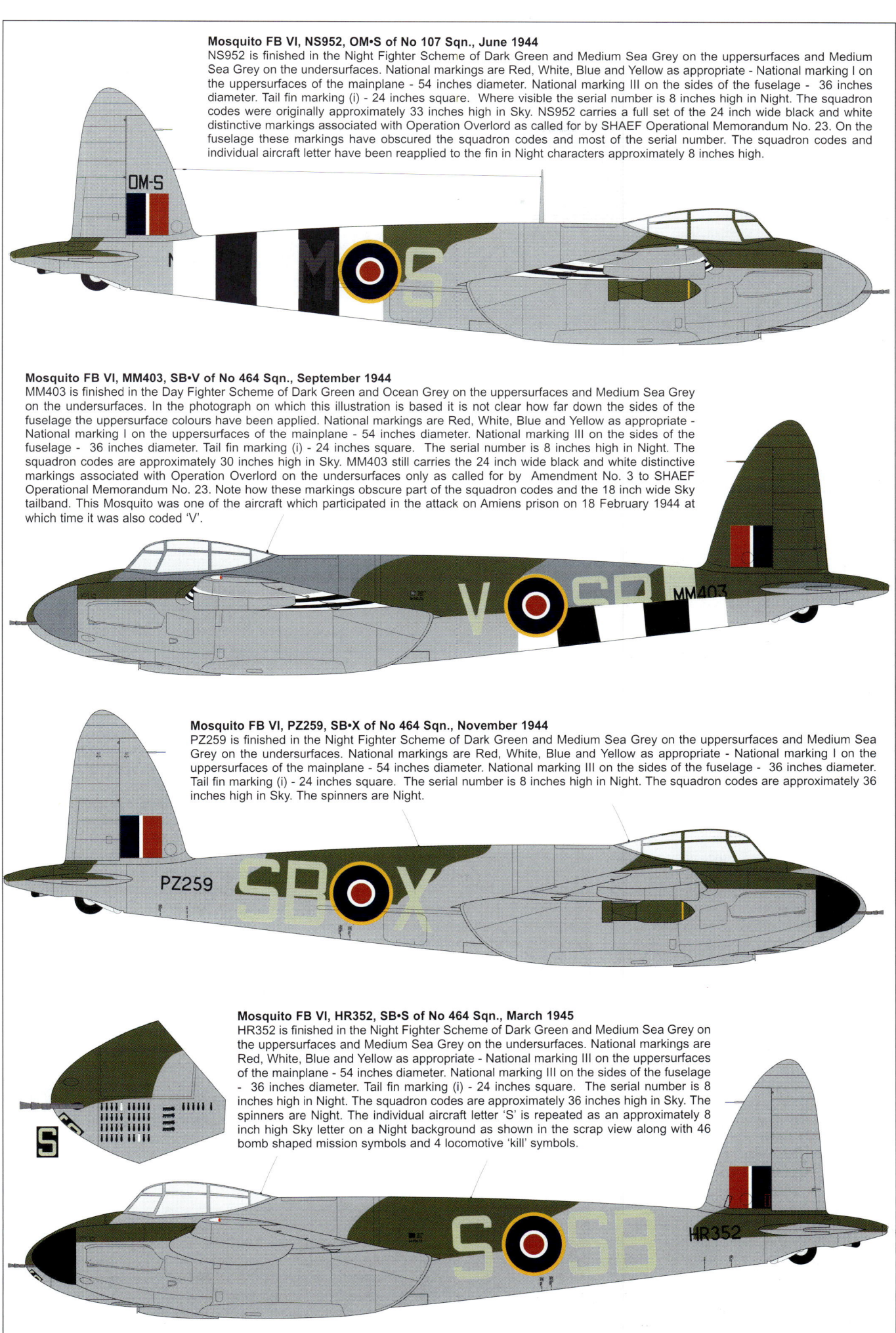

Mosquito FB VI, NS952, OM•S of No 107 Sqn., June 1944
NS952 is finished in the Night Fighter Scheme of Dark Green and Medium Sea Grey on the uppersurfaces and Medium Sea Grey on the undersurfaces. National markings are Red, White, Blue and Yellow as appropriate - National marking I on the uppersurfaces of the mainplane - 54 inches diameter. National marking III on the sides of the fuselage - 36 inches diameter. Tail fin marking (i) - 24 inches square. Where visible the serial number is 8 inches high in Night. The squadron codes were originally approximately 33 inches high in Sky. NS952 carries a full set of the 24 inch wide black and white distinctive markings associated with Operation Overlord as called for by SHAEF Operational Memorandum No. 23. On the fuselage these markings have obscured the squadron codes and most of the serial number. The squadron codes and individual aircraft letter have been reapplied to the fin in Night characters approximately 8 inches high.

Mosquito FB VI, MM403, SB•V of No 464 Sqn., September 1944
MM403 is finished in the Day Fighter Scheme of Dark Green and Ocean Grey on the uppersurfaces and Medium Sea Grey on the undersurfaces. In the photograph on which this illustration is based it is not clear how far down the sides of the fuselage the uppersurface colours have been applied. National markings are Red, White, Blue and Yellow as appropriate - National marking I on the uppersurfaces of the mainplane - 54 inches diameter. National marking III on the sides of the fuselage - 36 inches diameter. Tail fin marking (i) - 24 inches square. The serial number is 8 inches high in Night. The squadron codes are approximately 30 inches high in Sky. MM403 still carries the 24 inch wide black and white distinctive markings associated with Operation Overlord on the undersurfaces only as called for by Amendment No. 3 to SHAEF Operational Memorandum No. 23. Note how these markings obscure part of the squadron codes and the 18 inch wide Sky tailband. This Mosquito was one of the aircraft which participated in the attack on Amiens prison on 18 February 1944 at which time it was also coded 'V'.

Mosquito FB VI, PZ259, SB•X of No 464 Sqn., November 1944
PZ259 is finished in the Night Fighter Scheme of Dark Green and Medium Sea Grey on the uppersurfaces and Medium Sea Grey on the undersurfaces. National markings are Red, White, Blue and Yellow as appropriate - National marking I on the uppersurfaces of the mainplane - 54 inches diameter. National marking III on the sides of the fuselage - 36 inches diameter. Tail fin marking (i) - 24 inches square. The serial number is 8 inches high in Night. The squadron codes are approximately 36 inches high in Sky. The spinners are Night.

Mosquito FB VI, HR352, SB•S of No 464 Sqn., March 1945
HR352 is finished in the Night Fighter Scheme of Dark Green and Medium Sea Grey on the uppersurfaces and Medium Sea Grey on the undersurfaces. National markings are Red, White, Blue and Yellow as appropriate - National marking III on the uppersurfaces of the mainplane - 54 inches diameter. National marking III on the sides of the fuselage - 36 inches diameter. Tail fin marking (i) - 24 inches square. The serial number is 8 inches high in Night. The squadron codes are approximately 36 inches high in Sky. The spinners are Night. The individual aircraft letter 'S' is repeated as an approximately 8 inch high Sky letter on a Night background as shown in the scrap view along with 46 bomb shaped mission symbols and 4 locomotive 'kill' symbols.

Part Three: Maritime Strike

The first Mosquito squadron to form in Coastal Command other than the Photographic Reconnaissance Units, was also one of the most unusual and interesting of all the Mosquito squadrons. No 618 Squadron was formed on 1 April 1943 with the intention of attacking the German battleship *Tirpitz* with a weapon called 'Highball' which like the better known 'Upkeep' used by 617 Sqn on the Dams Raid, was a bouncing bomb designed by Barnes Wallis.

The original intention of the planners responsible for bringing Highball into service was that two squadrons would form, one in the UK and one in the Mediterranean, so sixty Mosquito B IVs were earmarked for conversion to carry two Highballs each.

It is thought that these aircraft were delivered in the standard Mosquito Bomber scheme of Dark Green and Ocean Grey on the upper surfaces with Medium Sea Grey on the under surfaces and carried the standard national markings and serial number in the usual positions. Some of the early deliveries to the squadron also carried a forward slash followed by the letter 'G' after the serial number to show that the aircraft was to be guarded at all times if it landed away from its home base, but this practice seems to have ceased on later aircraft.

Because Coastal Command had abandoned the two letter squadron code system in November 1942, no codes were allocated to 618 Sqn who marked their aircraft with only the individual aircraft letter on the sides of the fuselage, apparently in Sky.

The attack on the *Tirpitz*, never materialised and ultimately the idea of forming a second squadron was dropped. No 618 Squadron was subsequently despatched to Australia where it was hoped that 'Highball' could be used against the Japanese. No 618 Squadron's camouflage and markings whilst in Australia will be considered in the next chapter dealing with Mosquitoes in the Far East.

Whilst deliberations as to what should be done with 618 Squadron were going on, moves were afoot to alter the camouflage of some of Coastal Command's other aircraft. Operational experience had shown that the largely white colour scheme currently applied to Beaufighters operating off the Norwegian coast was too prominent and it was requested that the colour of the under surfaces of such aircraft should be repainted in what the correspondence on the matter seen by the author describes as a 'pale blue' or alternatively 'duck egg blue'.

On 8 September 1943, HQ Coastal Command wrote to 18 Group to say that there was no objection to a change in the camouflage of aircraft operating off the Norwegian coast being carried out, and instructions to this effect were evidently issued as on 6 October 1943.

18 Group once again wrote the HQ Coastal Command to inform them that it had been pointed out to the Group HQ by the Officer Commanding No 333 (Norwegian) Squadron that the existing under surfaces of Mosquito aircraft delivered to the squadron were painted in a "......matt light sea grey" and that he considered this colour to be as good a camouflage as 'duck egg blue', particularly as the grey toned in well with

Heading: Mosquito FB VI, PZ446 of 235 Sqn., circa autumn 1944. PZ446 is finished in the Special Coastal Duties Scheme A with AEAF black and white stripes under the rear fuselage only. In order to accommodate these markings, the serial number has been re-arranged with the two letters above the three numbers on the rear fuselage.

Right: Mosquito F II, DZ700 'H' of B Flight No 333 Sqn., circa late 1943. Finished in the Night Fighter Scheme of Dark Green and Medium Sea Grey, DZ700's single code letter 'H' appears to have been applied in Red. The Medium Sea Grey under surfaces were considered to tone in well with the colour of the Norwegian coastline that the Squadron operated over, but permission to retain this colour was refused by HQ Coastal Command.

Right: Mosquito FB VI, HR414, NE·L of 143 Sqn., circa December 1944. HR414 is finished in Special Coastal Duties Scheme A and had previously carried black and white AEAF 'invasion stripes' all the way around the rear fuselage as indicated by the darker band of fresh Extra Dark Sea Grey between the fuselage roundel and the tailplane, and the re-located code letters forward of the roundel plus the two prefix letters which have been moved above the three numbers of the serial number.

the colour of the Norwegian shore line. It was therefore requested that permission be given for Mosquito aircraft to retain this finish on the under surfaces in order to save the labour and material in repainting the under surfaces 'duck egg blue'.

HQ Coastal Command's reply of 13 October 1943 did not approve the retention of the grey on the under surfaces of 333 Squadron's Mosquitoes because it was thought that they might be required to reinforce No 16 or 19 Groups at any time where conditions were quite different.

Return to two-letter codes

With the growth of importance in the operations carried out by Coastal Command's Strike Wings, the Command began to rue the day it agreed to give up the two-letter squadron codes. In place of these two-letter codes, Coastal Command had instituted a system whereby each squadron on a Station was allocated a number as its squadron marking, eg 1, 2, or 3.

A consequence of this was found to be that when aircraft from different Stations operated together, there was often more than one aircraft with the same letter/number combination marked upon it in the formation. This led to difficulties in identification and the exercise of adequate tactical control of a large number of aircraft, which all looked very similar with no easy means of identifying one from another.

Sometime in the autumn of 1943 therefore, it would appear that Coastal Command sought and obtained Air Ministry approval to reinstate the two-letter squadron codes, as on 19 October 1943, Cypher AO/24 was sent from HQ Coastal Command to all its operational Groups to inform them that approval in principle had been obtained for the re-introduction of squadron identification code letters where the tactical operation of aircraft rendered it imperative. The Groups were invited to put forward the identity numbers of the squadrons under their jurisdiction who required such codes so that the new letters could be allotted by the Air Ministry.

Right: Mosquito FB VI, HR118, 3·W of 235 Sqn., June 1944. HR118 is finished in Special Coastal Duties Scheme A with a full set of the distinctive markings called for 'Operation Overlord' by SHAEF Operational Memorandum No 23. Interestingly, this Mosquito carries a numeral 3 as its squadron code under the Coastal Command system which assigned the numbers 1, 2 and 3 on a station by station basis. Note the 'staggered' serial number and what appear to be Red spinners.

Coastal Command's strike squadrons which ultimately equipped with Mosquitoes before the end of the war in Europe were allocated the following letters:-

143 Sqn: NE - This was a new code; previously the squadron had used the letters HO.
235 Sqn: LA - This was the same code the squadron had used previously.
248 Sqn: DM - This was a new code, previously the squadron had used the letters WR which are also known to have been used on the Mosquitoes.
254 Sqn: QM - This was a new code, previously the squadron had used the letters QY.
333 Sqn: KK - This was a new code as the squadron had not used codes previously.
404 Sqn: EO - This was a new code, previously the squadron had used the codes EE.

For some reason, when 235 Sqn equipped with Mosquitoes in June 1944, some of their aircraft are known to have been coded using the, by then, obsolete number system, carrying the number '3' as the squadron code in what appears to be Red.

Maritime strike scheme

On 3 November 1943 the definitive new Coastal Command camouflage scheme for strike aircraft was promulgated by Postagram from the Air Ministry. Upper and side surfaces were now to be Extra Dark Sea Grey with Sky under surfaces and standard national markings. At first this scheme was only applied to Beaufighters, but by 15 December 1943 arrangements had been made for Mosquito aircraft allocated to Coastal Command to be painted by 41 Group Maintenance Command in the same Extra Dark Sea Grey and Sky camouflage scheme.

The new camouflage scheme was applied over the top of the Medium Sea Grey and Dark Green Night Fighter Scheme applied on the production line. Some photographs illustrate this by showing that the serial number on the rear fuselage has been masked out and sprayed around, leaving the Night characters on an oblong background of the original factory applied colour. On the port side of the fuselage, the serial number lies on a background of Dark Green, whilst on the starboard side the serial number lies on a Medium Sea Grey background.

The new Coastal Command camouflage scheme for strike aircraft was finally incorporated into DTD Technical Circular 360 issue 2 in March 1944, when Special Coastal Duties Scheme A was amended to be Extra Dark Sea Grey and Sky to Pattern No 1, with Extra Dark Sea Grey spinners and no additional recognition markings. Serial numbers were to be Night and the roundels were to be standard National marking I on the upper surfaces of the

Mosquito FB VI, RS625, NE·D of 143 Sqn., whilst operating as part of the Banff Wing in the spring of 1945. RS625 was originally delivered to the Service in the Night Fighter Scheme of Dark Green and Medium Sea Grey. This scheme was then overpainted by 41 Group Maintenance Command in Special Coastal Duties Scheme A as called for by Amendment No 1 to DTD Technical Circular 360 Issue No 2 of 30 March 1944. This called for the upper surfaces to be finished in Extra Dark Sea Grey and the under surfaces in Sky to Pattern No 1. The original Night Fighter Scheme can still be seen where the Night serial number was masked out as the port side view shows the serial number on a Dark Green background, and the starboard side view shows the serial on a Medium Sea Grey background. The spinners were Yellow with Medium Sea Grey tips and bands whilst the codes were Night with Yellow outlines. Note the National marking IA on the upper surface of the mainplane which was introduced in January 1945 and the light coloured panel on the engine cowling. This latter feature is thought to be a treated but unpainted metal finish. The banked away view of RS625 shows the extent of the Sky under surfaces and the Banff Wing's armament in the spring of 1945 to advantage. The tiered rockets seen here were introduced at the end of February/beginning of March 1945. The rockets were Dark Green and the 100 gallon slipper tanks were silver, although it is not clear if this was a painted finish or not. The rocket and guard rails were natural metal.

scope of the memo which was to become effective on the day of the assault and thereafter until it was deemed advisable to change.

As the character and chronology of these markings has already been described and there is no need to repeat the information here. It should be remembered however that a wide variety of markings could be seen on Mosquitoes during the late summer and early autumn of 1944 which might range from a full set of distinctive markings to just having them on the underside of the rear fuselage.

In Coastal Command, the application of the stripes to the fuselage caused something of an upset as they obscured both the serial number and the tactically important squadron markings. The solution to this problem which was applied to many, although not all Mosquitoes seems to have been to move both markings.

The serial number was repositioned slightly so that the two prefix letters sat above the three numbers which remained in roughly the same place on the rear fuselage, whilst the squadron codes and individual aircraft letter were all moved forward of the roundel and repositioned near the top of the fuselage with the squadron codes separated from the individual aircraft letter by a hyphen in some cases.

The best known examples of these kinds of markings are to be found in the Banff Wing, which not only moved its Squadron Codes but also applied them in a variety of colours. Unfortunately, it is not possible to state with any degree of certainty exactly which colours were used by all the squadrons. No 143 Squadron is known to have used Night letters with

wings and National marking III on the fuselage. Tail fin marking (i) was applied to the fin.

It may be recalled that SHAEF Operational Memorandum No 23 first began to be circulated in April 1944. The stated object of this memorandum was to describe the distinctive black and white markings which were applied to aircraft of the United States and Britain in order to make them more easily identified as 'friendly' by ground and naval forces as well as by other friendly aircraft.

Coastal Command aircraft were amongst those aircraft specifically cited in the paragraph which dealt with the

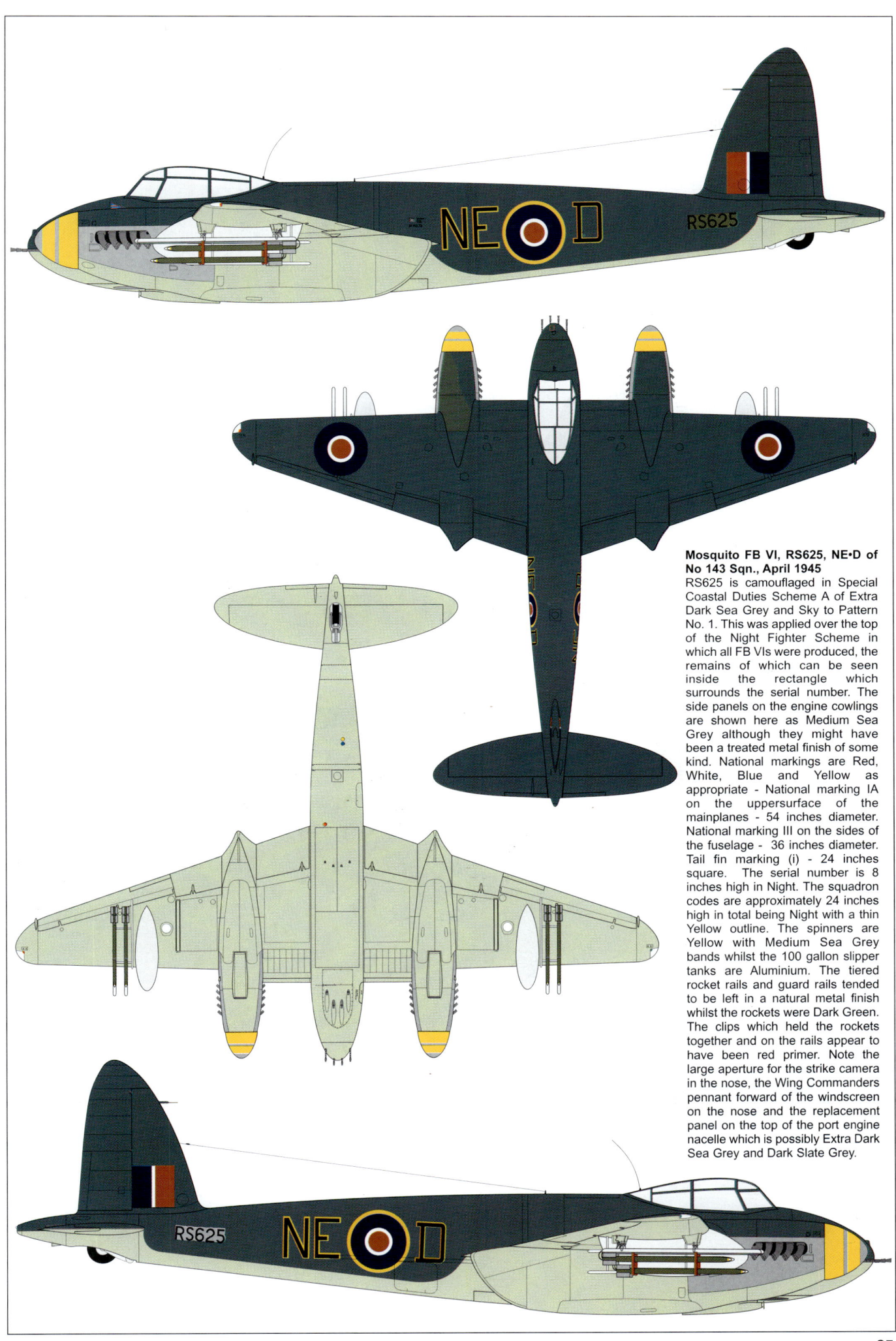

Mosquito FB VI, RS625, NE•D of No 143 Sqn., April 1945

RS625 is camouflaged in Special Coastal Duties Scheme A of Extra Dark Sea Grey and Sky to Pattern No. 1. This was applied over the top of the Night Fighter Scheme in which all FB VIs were produced, the remains of which can be seen inside the rectangle which surrounds the serial number. The side panels on the engine cowlings are shown here as Medium Sea Grey although they might have been a treated metal finish of some kind. National markings are Red, White, Blue and Yellow as appropriate - National marking IA on the uppersurface of the mainplanes - 54 inches diameter. National marking III on the sides of the fuselage - 36 inches diameter. Tail fin marking (i) - 24 inches square. The serial number is 8 inches high in Night. The squadron codes are approximately 24 inches high in total being Night with a thin Yellow outline. The spinners are Yellow with Medium Sea Grey bands whilst the 100 gallon slipper tanks are Aluminium. The tiered rocket rails and guard rails tended to be left in a natural metal finish whilst the rockets were Dark Green. The clips which held the rockets together and on the rails appear to have been red primer. Note the large aperture for the strike camera in the nose, the Wing Commanders pennant forward of the windscreen on the nose and the replacement panel on the top of the port engine nacelle which is possibly Extra Dark Sea Grey and Dark Slate Grey.

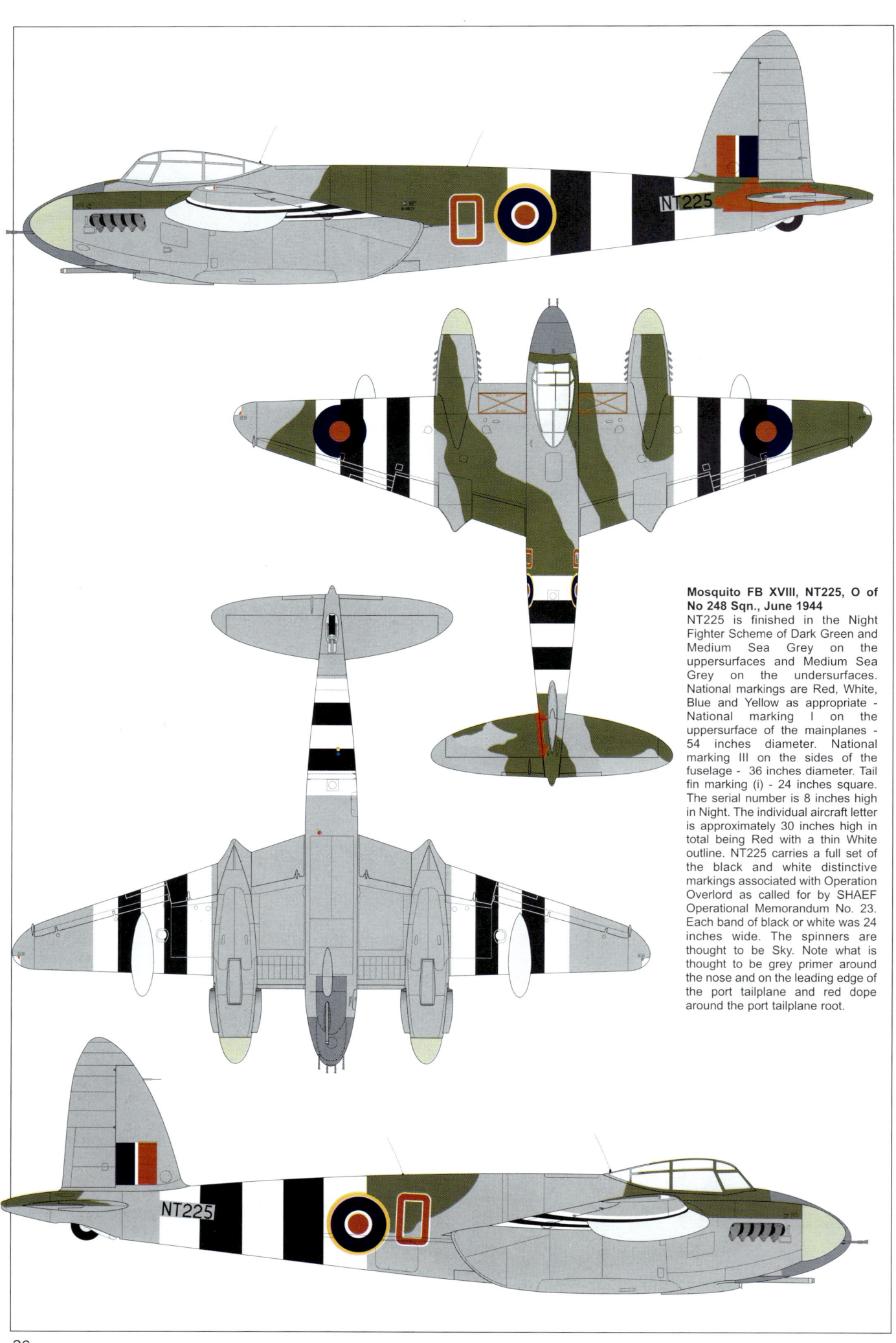

Mosquito FB XVIII, NT225, O of No 248 Sqn., June 1944

NT225 is finished in the Night Fighter Scheme of Dark Green and Medium Sea Grey on the uppersurfaces and Medium Sea Grey on the undersurfaces. National markings are Red, White, Blue and Yellow as appropriate - National marking I on the uppersurface of the mainplanes - 54 inches diameter. National marking III on the sides of the fuselage - 36 inches diameter. Tail fin marking (i) - 24 inches square. The serial number is 8 inches high in Night. The individual aircraft letter is approximately 30 inches high in total being Red with a thin White outline. NT225 carries a full set of the black and white distinctive markings associated with Operation Overlord as called for by SHAEF Operational Memorandum No. 23. Each band of black or white was 24 inches wide. The spinners are thought to be Sky. Note what is thought to be grey primer around the nose and on the leading edge of the port tailplane and red dope around the port tailplane root.

Above: Mosquito FB XVIII, NT225 'O' of 248 Sqn., in June 1944. NT225 carries a full set of the distinctive markings as called for by SHAEF Operational Memorandum No 23. Otherwise NT225, a so-called 'Tsetse' Mosquito, is finished in the standard Night Fighter Scheme with a Red individual aircraft letter which has a White outline. The barrel of the Mollins Gun carried by this type is visible under the nose and it is interesting to note that only two Brownings are carried, presumably as a weight saving measure.

Below right: Mosquito FB VI, RS568, VV·Z, thought to belong to the Sumburgh Station Flight, following a forced landing in Sweden in May 1945. This photograph is of interest because of the unusual VV code which has been attributed to Sumburgh Station Flight, but has been applied in the same manner as used by the Banff Wing. Whilst the colours are not known for certain, they may be Blue with a Yellow outline, or alternatively Night with a Yellow outline, which was the combination used by No 143 Sqn.

a thin Yellow outline on some aircraft, but alternatively plain Yellow letters on others and to also have decorated its spinners with Yellow.

No 235 Sqn used a very light colour, such as White or Sky, with a red outline and is said to have had red spinners. The exact shade of red is open to question as a colour photograph of Max Aitken's HR366, thought to have been coded 'O1', which is said to have been on the charge of 235 Sqn clearly shows it to have had Bright Red spinners.

No 404 Sqn used a dark colour such as Blue or Night with what appears to be a White outline with White spinners.

No 248 Sqn appears to have originally applied the codes WR in red with white outlines but when these codes were replaced by the letters DM, the new codes appear to have used a darker colour, again possibly Blue or Night. This unknown colour was also applied to the spinners which had what is thought to be White tips. Perhaps the most likely colour would have been Night as it is known that Beaufighters finished in the Extra Dark Sea Grey and Sky scheme had their codes letters applied in Night

Coastal Command's Mosquitoes were amongst those aircraft affected by Cypher AX 110 dated 2 January 1945, from the Air Ministry to all RAF Command Headquarters at home and overseas which gave notice that with effect from 7 January 1945, all aircraft other than those whose primary role was night operations, and aircraft operating in Air Command South East Asia and the Pacific were to revert to Red, White, and Blue roundels on the upper surfaces of the mainplanes in place of the Red and Blue National marking I as previously described.

As far as is known, no further changes were made to the camouflage and markings of Coastal Command's Mosquitoes before the end of the war in Europe, although it is possible that the application of Special Coastal Duties Scheme A began to be considered less essential in the last few months of the war as several Mosquitoes seem to have retained, or even to have been re-painted in, the Night Fighter Scheme and the use of Night codes seems to have become more widespread.

Left: Mosquito FB VI, RF838, EO·A of 404 Sqn., circa April 1945. RF838 appears to have been repainted in the Night Fighter Scheme from the Special Coastal Duties Scheme A as indicated by the darker colour which surrounds the serial number on the rear fuselage. Why this was done is not known but the Mosquito in the background is also in the Night Fighter Scheme, so RF838 may not have been the only example on the Squadron. Note the coloured codes on the fuselage, (possibly Night with a Yellow outline?), National marking IAs on the upper surface of the wings and the tiered rockets.

Mosquito B IV, DZ582/G, U of No 618 Sqn., circa May 1943
DZ582 is finished in the Day Fighter Scheme of Dark Green and Ocean Grey uppersurfaces with Medium Sea Grey undersurfaces and Ocean Grey spinners. National markings are Red, White, Blue and Yellow as appropriate - National marking I on the uppersurfaces of the mainplane - 54 inches diameter. National marking III on the sides of the fuselage - 36 inches diameter. Tail fin marking (i) - 24 inches square. The serial number is 8 inches high in Night. Because 618 Sqn formed after Coastal Command abandoned the two letter squadron codes no codes were ever allocated to the Squadron whilst it was serving in the UK. As a consequence, only the individual aircraft letter was carried, in this case being approximately 24 inches high in Sky.

Mosquito FB VI, HP862, KK•K of No 333 Sqn., circa summer 1943
HP862 is finished in the Night Fighter Scheme of Dark Green and Medium Sea Grey on the uppersurfaces and Medium Sea Grey on the undersurfaces. National markings are Red, White, Blue and Yellow as appropriate - National marking I on the uppersurfaces of the mainplane - 54 inches diameter. National marking III on the sides of the fuselage - 36 inches diameter. Tail fin marking (i) - 24 inches square. The serial number is 8 inches high in Night. The squadron codes are approximately 30 inches high in Sky. Note the small Norwegian flag which was applied to the port side of the nose.

Mosquito FB VI, HR118, 3•W of No 235 Sqn., June 1944
HR118 is camouflaged in Special Coastal Duties Scheme A of Extra Dark Sea Grey and Sky to Pattern No. 1. This was applied over the top of the Night Fighter Scheme in which all FB VIs were produced. National markings are Red, White, Blue and Yellow as appropriate - National marking I on the uppersurface of the mainplanes - 54 inches diameter. National marking III on the sides of the fuselage - 36 inches diameter. Tail fin marking (i) - 24 inches square. The serial number is 8 inches high in Night. This aircraft is a rare example of a Mosquito apparently using the Coastal Command system of using numbers as squadron codes on a station by station basis, in this case the number '3' which is approximately 15 inches high in Red. The individual aircraft letter 'W' is approximately 30 inches high also in Red. HR118 carries a full set of the 24 inch wide black and white stripes which make up the distinctive markings associated with Operation Overlord as called for by SHAEF Operational Memorandum No. 23. On the fuselage these markings have obscured the original serial number layout which has led to the serial number being reapplied with the two letters above the three numbers as shown. The spinners are Red.

Mosquito FB VI, LR347, T of No 235 Sqn., June 1944
LR347 is camouflaged in Special Coastal Duties Scheme A of Extra Dark Sea Grey and Sky to Pattern No. 1. National markings are Red, White, Blue and Yellow as appropriate - National marking I on the uppersurface of the mainplanes - 54 inches diameter. National marking III on the sides of the fuselage - 36 inches diameter. Tail fin marking (i) - 24 inches square. The serial number is 8 inches high in Night. This Mosquito might have been originally marked using the Coastal Command system of using numbers as squadron codes on a station by station basis, in this case the number '3'. However, the photograph on which this illustration has been based shows clear signs of having whatever marking was forward of the roundel painted out. The individual aircraft letter 'T' is approximately 24 inches high in Red. LR347 carries a full set of the black and white distinctive markings associated with Operation Overlord as called for by SHAEF Operational Memorandum No. 23. On the fuselage these markings have obscured the original serial number layout which has led to the serial number being reapplied over the top of the markings slightly lower down the side of the fuselage than normal. The spinners are Red.

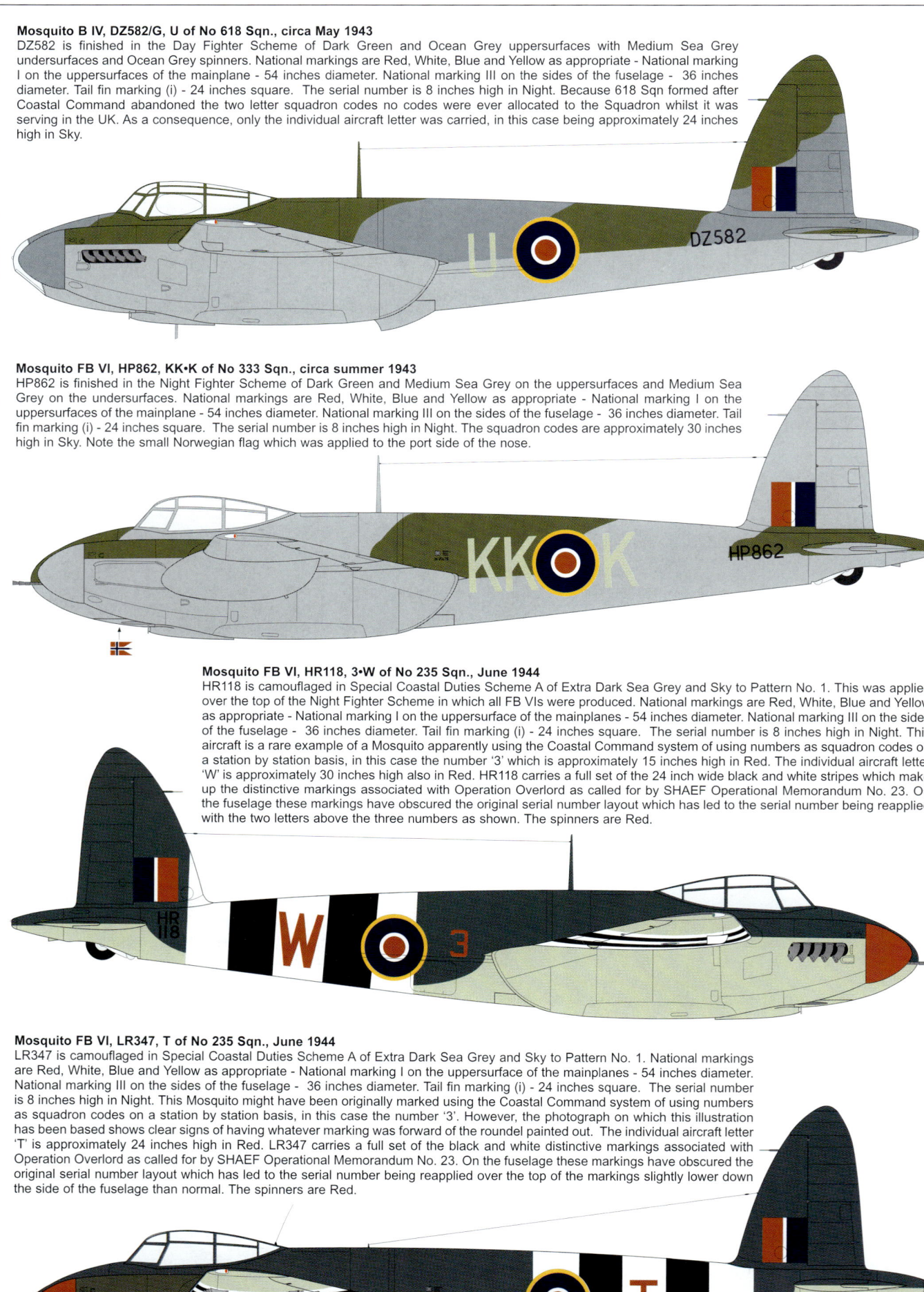

Mosquito FB VI, HR130, LA•E of No 235 Sqn., circa winter 1944/45
HR130 is camouflaged in Special Coastal Duties Scheme A of Extra Dark Sea Grey and Sky to Pattern No. 1. National markings are Red, White, Blue and Yellow as appropriate - National marking I or possibly IA on the uppersurface of the mainplanes - 54 inches diameter. National marking III on the sides of the fuselage - 36 inches diameter. Tail fin marking (i) - 24 inches square. The serial number is 8 inches high in Night. HR130 still carries the 24 inch wide black and white distinctive markings associated with Operation Overlord on the undersurfaces only as called for by Amendment No. 3 to SHAEF Operational Memorandum No. 23. Note how these markings have been applied around the serial number on the rear fuselage and how the squadron codes have been moved to avoid them altogether. On HR130 the codes appear to have been applied in White with a thin Yellow outline, but this practice is thought to have been varied on other aircraft in the squadron. These codes are approximately 24 inches high in total. The spinners are Red

Mosquito FB VI, RF610, DM•H of No 248 Sqn., circa spring 1945
RF610 is camouflaged in Special Coastal Duties Scheme A of Extra Dark Sea Grey and Sky to Pattern No. 1. The side panels on the engine cowlings are shown here as Medium Sea Grey though they might have been a treated metal finish of some kind. National markings are Red, White, Blue and Yellow as appropriate - National marking IA on the uppersurface of the mainplanes - 54 inches diameter. National marking III on the sides of the fuselage - 36 inches diameter. Tail fin marking (i) - 24 inches square. The serial number is 8 inches high in Night. The squadron codes are approximately 24 inches high in Night. The spinners are Night with what are thought to be White tips whilst the 100 gallon slipper tanks are Aluminium. The tiered rocket rails and guard rails tended to be left in a natural metal finish whilst the rockets were Dark Green. The clips which held the rockets together and on the rails appear to have been red primer.

Mosquito FB XVIIII, PZ468, QM•D of No 254 Sqn., circa spring 1945
PZ468 is finished in the Night Fighter Scheme of Dark Green and Medium Sea Grey on the uppersurfaces and Medium Sea Grey on the undersurfaces. National markings are Red, White, Blue and Yellow as appropriate - National marking IA on the uppersurfaces of the mainplane - 54 inches diameter. National marking III on the sides of the fuselage - 36 inches diameter. Tail fin marking (i) - 24 inches square. The serial number is 8 inches high in Night. The squadron codes are approximately 30 inches high in Night. The spinners are Medium Sea Grey with White bands. Note the slightly darker area under the rear fuselage where the black and white distinctive markings have been overpainted.

Mosquito FB VI, RF838, ED•A of No 404 Sqn., circa spring 1945
RF838 is finished in the Night Fighter Scheme of Dark Green and Medium Sea Grey on the uppersurfaces and Medium Sea Grey on the undersurfaces. National markings are Red, White, Blue and Yellow as appropriate - National marking IA on the uppersurfaces of the mainplane - 54 inches diameter. National marking III on the sides of the fuselage - 36 inches diameter. Tail fin marking (i) - 24 inches square. The serial number is 8 inches high in Night. The squadron codes are thought to be Night with a thin White outline approximately 24 inches high in total. The spinners are White. The 100 gallon slipper tanks are Aluminium. The tiered rocket rails and guard rails tended to be left in a natural metal finish whilst the rockets were Dark Green. The clips which held the rockets together and on the rails appear to have been red primer.

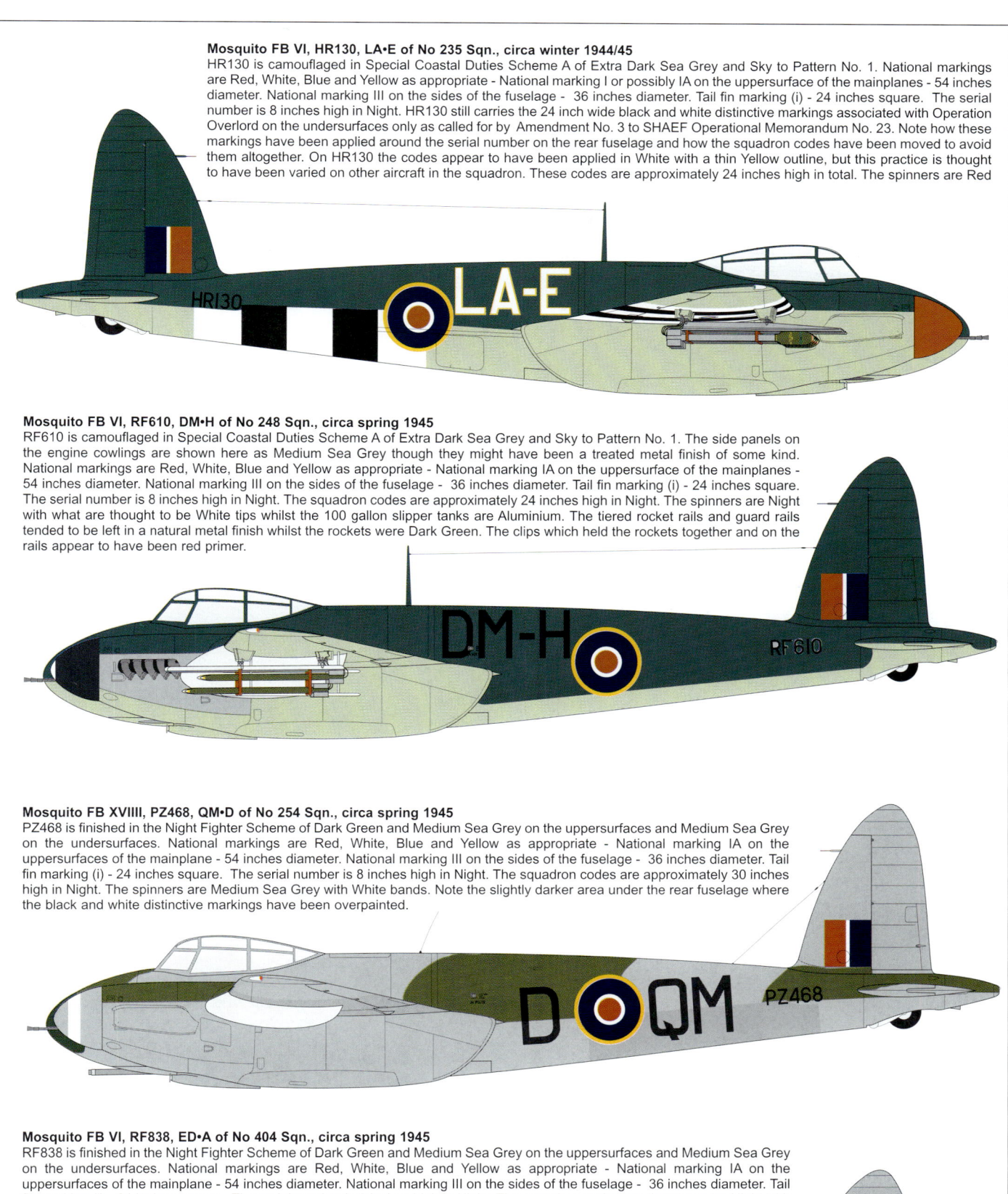

Part Four: Mosquitoes in the Far East

In January 1944, the Air Ministry planned to equip over twenty squadrons in ACSEA with the Mosquito, but this plan slowly unravelled in the face of technical problems with the aircraft despite the strenuous attempts made by both de Havillands and the MAP to overcome them.

Early deliveries of Mosquito FB VIs to the Far East are thought to have retained their European 'grey and green' camouflage schemes for a time. Photographic evidence suggests that Mosquitoes were despatched to the Far East in both the Day Fighter and the Night Fighter Schemes. Mosquitoes in both of these schemes were photographed both with and without Sky spinners and tailbands.

By the time that the first Fighter-Bomber Mosquitoes to serve in the Far East, the Mosquito FB VIs of 45 Sqn.,

Heading: Two Mosquito FB VIs of 47 Sqn., in the overall Aluminium finish in 1945. Note the 'skull and cross bones' motif on the crew access door and individual aircraft letter 'V' on the nose under the four 0.303 inch Brownings of the nearest Mosquito. These markings, like the spinners might be Night or Blue in colour.

Right: Mosquito FB VI, HP877, shortly after its delivery flight to the Far East, finished in the Night Fighter Scheme of Dark Green and Medium Sea Grey with European Theatre National markings. Note the word 'SNAKE' on the rear fuselage which was applied to aircraft being sent to the Far East to signify to any Operational Command through whose jurisdiction the aircraft might pass, that the aircraft was not to be impressed for service anywhere along its route!

began operations in September 1945, the camouflage and marking of RAF aircraft in the Far East was laid down in Air Force Orders (India) Nos 69-76, dated 4 April 1944.

These orders stated that the camouflage schemes for the various types of aircraft which had been tabulated in AMO A.664/42 as amended by AMOs A.1096/42 and A.1377/42, held good for aircraft in the Far East with a few exceptions which were then listed.

National markings

The first exception which applied to Mosquitoes lay in the application of National markings. Air Force Orders (India) Nos 69-76 specified that the National markings given in AMO A.664/42, (ie National markings I, II and III with their associated fin marking), had been superseded by those set out in AFO (India) 357/43 which gave details of identification markings which had been designed to prevent confusion with the Japanese *Hinomaru* national marking.

From the outbreak of hostilities in the Far East in December 1941, the prominence of the Red centre in the British national marking had proved a problem as the Blue colour often faded to the point where at a distance it merged in to the camouflage. As a result, the Red centre became the most prominent feature of the marking, thus offering ample scope for mis-identification for the Japanese national marking.

The Royal Australian Air Force was the first to recognise the problem and to do something about it, revising their national marking to remove the red from it during the summer of 1942. By 23 April 1943,

Right: Mosquito FB VI, HJ770, circa late 1944, also appears to be finished in the Night Fighter Scheme - but unusually also has Sky spinners and tailband. 'SNAKE' appears in Night just above the serial number on the rear fuselage.

the problem of the Red in British national markings had become so acute that a proposal was put forward by AHQ Bengal to AHQ India that the British national markings carried by RAF aircraft in that Theatre should be altered.

The problem was that with an increasing amount of co-operation taking place between the British and Americans, the Americans were experiencing difficulty in recognising British aircraft due to the fading of the identification markings on the upper surfaces of the mainplanes. This problem was made worse by the inexperience of pilots and the similarity between the Mohawk which was extensively used by the RAF in India at that time and the Japanese A6M 'Zero'.

In its reply on 24 April 1943, AHQ India informed AHQ Bengal that no alteration of the National markings could be permitted. Instead, it was suggested that Mohawks, (and only the Mohawks), should adopt a Yellow band 6 inches wide on the upper surface of the mainplanes. This marking was suggested because it was known to have been effective when applied to Mustangs in the UK.

AHQ Bengal was not impressed, pointing out that an American General, General Haynes, had almost fallen victim to faulty identification whilst being flown in an RAF Hudson and was therefore taking some interest in the matter. AHQ India was requested to reconsider its decision. Clearly the American interest in the question of altering the national markings was too much of a political 'hot potato' for India Command, and it referred the matter to the Air Ministry on 29 April 1943.

AHQ India suggested that the national markings could be made more distinctive by re-introducing the Yellow outer ring to the roundels on the upper surfaces of the mainplanes. The Air Ministry replied on 11 May, suggesting that markings similar to those adopted by the Royal Australian Air Force in the Pacific Theatre should be adopted which consisted of a white centre surrounded by a blue ring, thus eliminating red from the national markings altogether.

AHQ India agreed to this suggestion on 15 May, and asked for the Air Ministry's approval before instituting the change. As no reply had been received by 24 June, AHQ India authorised the change anyway and informed the Air Ministry accordingly.

Trials were put in hand to assess the new marking's suitability, during which it was discovered that the white centre in the new roundel was too prominent and compromised the camouflage of the aircraft. The solution was to mix a new off-white colour using four parts White and one part Blue, which was found to give a marking which was visible from 1,700 yards but did not compromise the aircraft's camouflage scheme. At the same time the fin flash was also altered to off-white and Blue, with the off-white leading. Although this off-white colour appears to never have had an official name, it is convenient to refer to it as 'SEAC white'.

Introduced from the end of June 1943, the new markings were originally sized in accordance with the provisions of the then current AMO, but after the Australians had been consulted about their markings, the RAF adopted the same proportions as the markings employed by the RAAF from about September 1943.

The new National markings were designed for three sizes of aircraft, small, medium, and large, with the Mosquito being classed as a medium sized aircraft. Therefore they should have had Blue roundels of 32 inches overall diameter with 12 inch diameter 'SEAC white' centres and a fin flash 24 inches high and 22 inches wide divided into two 11 inch wide segments of Blue and 'SEAC white'. These markings then remained in use by SEAC for the rest of the war in the Far East. The roundels on the wing upper surfaces were supposed to be unaffected except that the Red centre was to be replaced with 'SEAC white', but it would appear that the small 32 inch roundel was often used instead, especially on Mosquitoes in the later Aluminium finish.

Camouflage finish

The second exception given by Air Force Orders (India) Nos 69-76 dated 4 April 1944, which applied to the Mosquito was the camouflage finish to be applied to Bomber aircraft. When the Mosquito FB VIs which had been despatched to the Far East began to be allocated to squadrons, they were used to replace the Vultee Vengeances of Nos 45, 47, 82, 84 and 110 Squadrons where they were apparently seen as *bomber* aircraft. This interpretation is supported by documents relating to the adoption of the overall Aluminium finish which consistently refer to the type as 'Mk VI LB', the 'LB' presumably meaning Light Bomber.

Uppersurface camouflage

Air Force Orders (India) Nos 69-76 dated 4 April 1944, called for the upper surfaces of Day Bombers to be in the Temperate Land Scheme of Dark Green and Dark Earth. When the FB VIs left the production line they were finished in the Night Fighter Scheme of Dark Green and Medium Sea Grey with the demarcation line between the upper and under surfaces running down the centre of the fuselage when seen in side elevation in the usual way.

Photographs of some Mosquito FB VIs in the Far East show that when the Dark Earth was added to the existing Dark Green by the Service in the Far East to meet the requirement for Temperate Land Scheme upper surfaces, either to the A or C schemes, this demarcation line was retained, whilst on other Mosquitoes, the upper surface colours were brought further down the sides of the fuselage to Pattern No 1.

Undersurface camouflage

Whilst Air Force Orders (India) Nos 69-76 dated 4 April 1944, called for the upper surfaces of Day Bombers to be in the Temperate Land Scheme, they made no mention of the under surfaces. This implies that the provisions of AMO A.664/42 and its amendments remained in force for the under surface of Day Bombers in the Far East. AMO A.664/42 gives the under surface colours to be used on the under surfaces of Day Bombers serving Overseas as 'Sky or azure'. It is the author's opinion that this last requirement actually means Sky *Blue* or Azure *Blue* and not Sky as this colour was rejected as being unsuitable for use in the Middle East in 1940.

Most of the black and white photographs seen by the author which appear to show Mosquitoes finished in the Temperate Land Scheme on the upper surfaces also appear to show the under surfaces to have been finished in a colour similar to the colour of the SEAC white centres to the roundels. SEAC white had an approximate diffuse reflectivity of 41 percent compared with Sky Blue's 52 percent, Azure Blue's 30 percent and Medium Sea Grey's 26 percent. It is therefore thought that most Mosquito FB VIs in the Far East had their Medium Sea Grey under surfaces repainted in Azure Blue which of the two colours specified in AMO A.664/42 saw the greatest use.

It is of interest to note that with a difference of only 4 percent in the diffuse

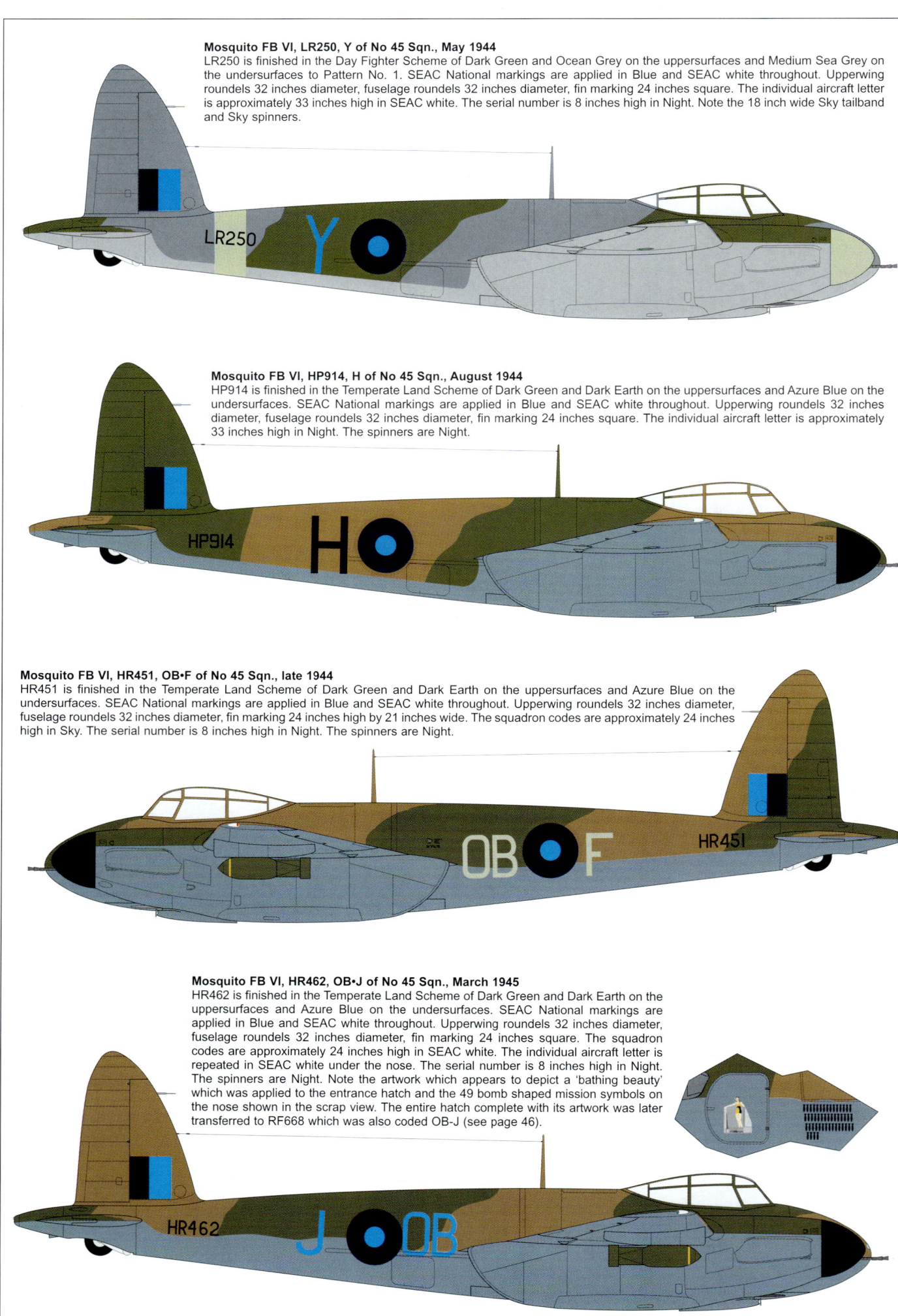

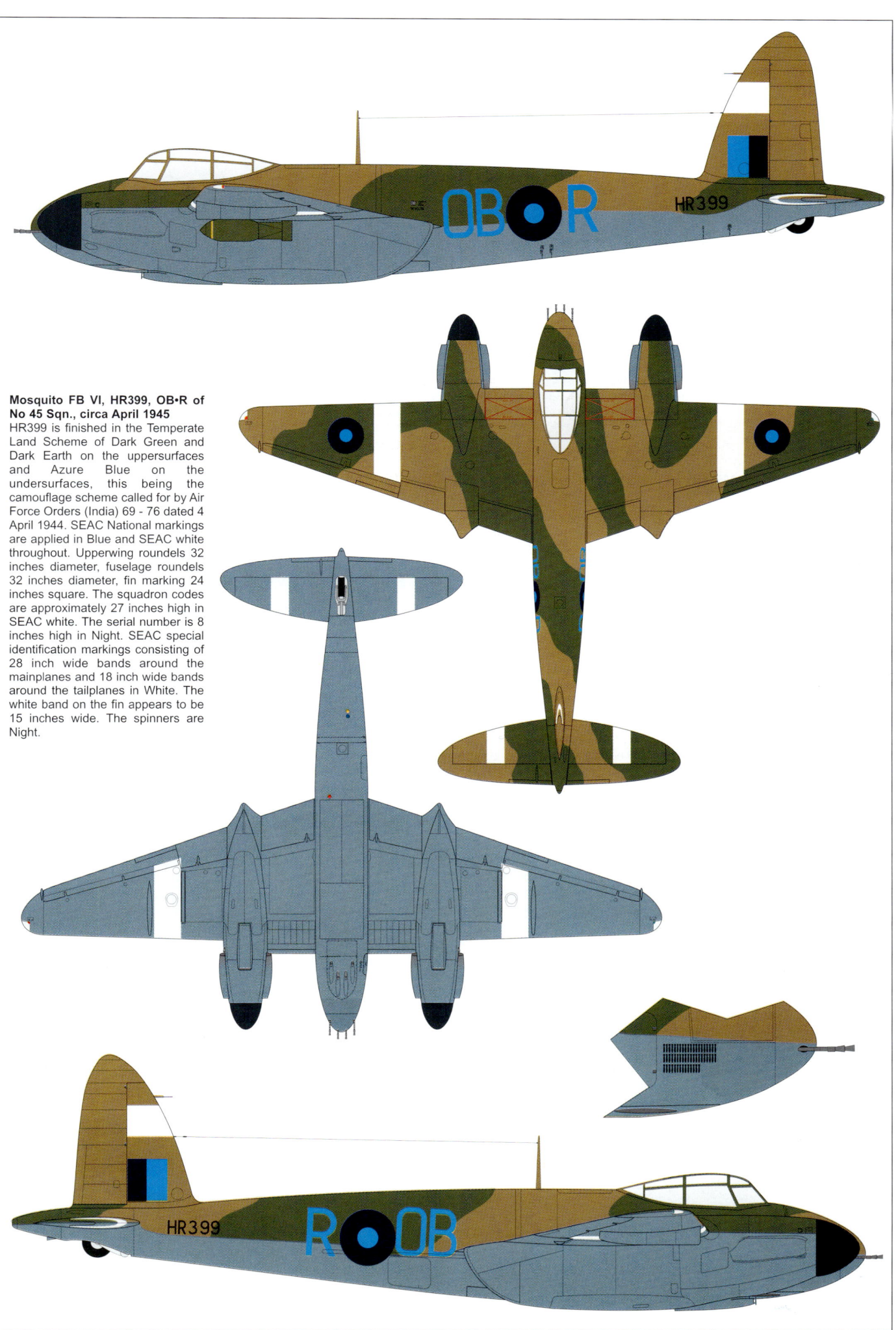

Mosquito FB VI, HR399, OB·R of No 45 Sqn., circa April 1945

HR399 is finished in the Temperate Land Scheme of Dark Green and Dark Earth on the uppersurfaces and Azure Blue on the undersurfaces, this being the camouflage scheme called for by Air Force Orders (India) 69 - 76 dated 4 April 1944. SEAC National markings are applied in Blue and SEAC white throughout. Upperwing roundels 32 inches diameter, fuselage roundels 32 inches diameter, fin marking 24 inches square. The squadron codes are approximately 27 inches high in SEAC white. The serial number is 8 inches high in Night. SEAC special identification markings consisting of 28 inch wide bands around the mainplanes and 18 inch wide bands around the tailplanes in White. The white band on the fin appears to be 15 inches wide. The spinners are Night.

Right: Mosquito FB VI, HR462, OB·J, of 45 Sqn., circa March 1945. This photograph shows that HR462 had its undersurfaces repainted from the original Medium Sea Grey with a slightly lighter colour, probably Azure Blue. The colour of the bomb symbols and the individual aircraft letter on the nose are unfortunately unknown.

reflectivity between Medium Sea Grey and Azure Blue, the two colours are probably indistinguishable unless both are present and in close proximity to each other on the same aircraft at the same time.

Circumstantial evidence which might suggest that many Mosquitoes might have had 'blue' under surfaces is provided by a report tendered to the MAP by a a representative of Imperial Chemical Industries (ICI) who made a tour of India towards the end of 1944 in order to examine the problems and practices of aircraft finishing in the Far East. At the time of the tour, the representative found the Temperate Land Scheme as described above in use and noted that in some instances it had been felt necessary to re-camouflage the under surfaces of an aircraft *because the shade of grey was incorrect* or had faded (emphasis added).

Further circumstantial evidence is provided by the Highball Mosquito B IVs of 618 Sqn which arrived in Australia early in 1945 which are known to have been finished with Azure Blue under surfaces. These aircraft will be dealt with in greater detail below.

Introduction of Aluminium

Problems with operating the Mosquito in the Far East began to manifest themselves on 20 October 1944 when a Mosquito of 82 Sqn., the second squadron to convert to the FB VI, lost half its starboard wing outboard of the engine whilst making a practice bombing attack. An investigating team led by Major de Havilland went out to India towards the end of November 1944 to investigate the problem. On his return in January 1945, Major de Havilland reported to the MAP that the wing failures could be attributed to water penetration, differential shrinkage of parts of the airframe structure due to high temperatures, and defective glue joints.

One of the recommendations Major de Havilland made to ACSEA on how the risks of structural failure could be reduced, was that the use of camouflage dopes should be abandoned and replaced with an Aluminium finish on all surfaces. On 20 January 1945 Air Command South East Asia (ACSEA) informed the Air Ministry of this advice and asked for future supplies of what are described as Mk VI LB and PR Mosquitoes to be given this finish.

Right: Mosquito FB VI, HR493 UX·C of 82 Sqn., circa late 1944. HR493 is thought to have been camouflaged in the Temperate Land Scheme on the upper surfaces and Azure Blue on the under surfaces, as called for by Air Force Orders (India) 69-76 in April 1944. All national markings are 'SEAC white' and Blue. The code letters appear to be Night.

However, work had been started in the UK to develop a new type of dope which would have greater heat resisting properties than those of DTD 83A, and part of the Air Ministry felt that it was not worth organising any change in the production line to an Aluminium finish at that time. However, on 24 January, the Air Ministry signalled ACSEA to suggest the use of glossy camouflage to DTD 63A, a pre-war gloss finish specification, as this offered an improvement over the matt finish, although not as great an improvement as would be bestowed by an Aluminium finish.

On 1 February 1945, ACSEA replied confirming its preference for the glossy Aluminium finish which was acknowledged by the Air Ministry on 4 February. At this stage it would appear that only day flying Mosquitoes were to be finished Aluminium. The NF XIXs which were due to be delivered to the Far East were not immediately affected.

Documents from the middle of February specifically state that no change was to be made in the camouflage of these aircraft at that time, but that special instructions would be issued later. However, by the end of February, the decision had been taken that all Mosquito NF XIX aircraft which were despatched to ACSEA would also be given an Aluminium finish. Most of the airframe was to be finished in Aluminium to DTD 63A whilst the control surfaces, ie the elevators, ailerons and rudder, were to be finished with Aluminium to DTD 83A.

This new finish does not appear to have been applied at the factory. It would appear that 41 Group Maintenance Command was given the task of applying two coats of the Aluminium finish over the camouflage finish which was applied on the production line, as otherwise production would have been disrupted.

Matters rested there until the summer, when on 18 July 1945, the Air Ministry signalled ACSEA to inform them that laboratory tests showed that the use of the new Infra-Red heat resisting dopes which were now available in camouflage colours and undercoats, would provide at least as much protection from heat and weather as the Aluminium finish now in use. The Air Ministry proposed an immediate reversion to camouflage using the new dopes.

ACSEA were not impressed. They had been conducting trials with the new finish at Cawnpore in India since late February, and on 30 July 1945, informed the Air Ministry that the laboratory findings were not confirmed under the Indian sun! The importance of retaining the Aluminium finish was stressed. Perhaps not surprisingly, this did not go down well at the Air Ministry as the aircraft finish industry was by this stage committed to producing the new Infra-Red resisting dopes to DTD Specifications 751-754 in large quantities.

Early August saw the Air Ministry 'going on to the offensive', questioning the methodology of ACSEA's trials and therefore the validity of their results, and pointing out the great amount of work entailed in finishing Mosquitoes in the

Aluminium finish outlined above and the potential drawbacks of doing so, citing delay in despatch, susceptibility to embrittlement of the finish, and the increased weight it would bestow.

Whilst agreeing that there was no question of condemning the use of the new dopes at this stage, ACSEA were still not prepared to accept all its Mosquitoes in this finish and suggested that the use of Aluminium should continue until further experience with the new dope was obtained because the Aluminium finish was known to have a beneficial effect.

By early September, the issue had become academic to some degree as with the surrender of Japan, the use of camouflage was no longer strictly necessary and the whole issue of aircraft camouflage for all RAF aircraft was under review. In the event, the new DTD 751-754 dopes became the post-war standard.

Identification markings

Although squadron codes had been abolished for most of the RAF in 1942, photographs of Mosquitoes serving with Nos 45 and 82 Squadrons show that both units continued to use their two letter codes until the end of the war on both Temperate Land Scheme and overall Aluminium finished Mosquitoes.

Air Force Orders (India) Nos 69-76, made no exception for the colour of the

Above: Mosquito FB VI, HR559, UX·X of 82 Sqn., 1945, finished in the overall Aluminium finish introduced from January 1945 with Air Command South East Asia's Blue special identification markings on the wings, tailplane and fin. The code letters and serial number, which is repeated on the fin, are in Night and the National markings are applied in 'SEAC white' and Blue. Note the use of the 32 inch diameter roundel for medium sized aircraft on both the upper surfaces of the wings and side of the fuselage.

Right: Mosquito FB VI, HR551, UX·P of 82 Sqn., circa February 1945. HR551 is also finished in overall Aluminium with ACSEA's special identification markings on the wings, tailplane and fin and rudder. These markings were to be 18 inches wide and to be Blue on Aluminium finished aircraft. Note that whilst the bands on the wings and tailplanes stop short of the ailerons and elevators, the band on the tail extends across the rudder.

squadron identification codes and the individual aircraft letter, implying that they should have been marked on Day Bombers in Red, but as Red was frowned upon for any kind of marking in the Far East, it would appear that other colours such as Sky, 'SEAC white' and Night were used on Mosquitoes finished in the Temperate Land Scheme whilst Night or Blue was used on Aluminium finished Mosquitoes.

Serial numbers were to be applied in Night, and this was indeed the norm on Mosquitoes in both the Temperate Land and overall Aluminium schemes. On some Aluminium finished aircraft, the serial number was repeated on the tailfin in characters approximately 3 inches high. The reason for this is not known.

Special identification markings

Air Command South East Asia employed its own special identification markings which on the Mosquito took the form of coloured spinners; a 28 inch wide band around the mainplanes; and 18 inch wide bands around the tailplanes and fins.

These markings were originally introduced in December 1944, on Thunderbolt aircraft following concerns that they might be mistaken for the Nakajima Ki 44-II *Shoki* fighter, but from 1 February 1945, were to be carried by all aircraft in ACSEA with the exception of Night Fighters and four engined aircraft.

The markings were to be applied in White on camouflaged aircraft and Blue on uncamouflaged aircraft, although the use of Night on uncamouflaged aircraft was not unknown by some units.

On 3 February 1945, the Air Ministry signalled ACSEA to voice its concern over the extent of these bands which it stated should not extend onto control surfaces ie elevators, ailerons and the rudder, due the possibility of upsetting the balance of the control surfaces. ACSEA were advised to standardise the markings on all aircraft to exclude the control surfaces. By this time however, the markings had already been applied to many aircraft and as a result aircraft could be seen both *with* and *without* these markings extending across their control surfaces.

On 9 March 1945, ACSEA wrote to the Air Ministry giving further details of its special identity markings. As from 10 March 1945, only Fighters, ie P-38 Lightnings, P-47 Thunderbolts, P-51 Mustangs, Spitfires, Hurricanes and Tactical Reconnaissance aircraft were to carry the markings. Thus from this date Mosquito FB VIs were no longer to be marked, although it would appear that those Mosquitoes which already had the markings continued to carry them.

618 Sqn in Australia

The Highball-equipped Mosquito B IVs of No 618 Squadron were covered in detail in Combat Colours No 5, **'The de Havilland Mosquito in RAF Photographic Reconnaissance and Bomber service: 1941 to 1945'**, to which interested readers are referred.

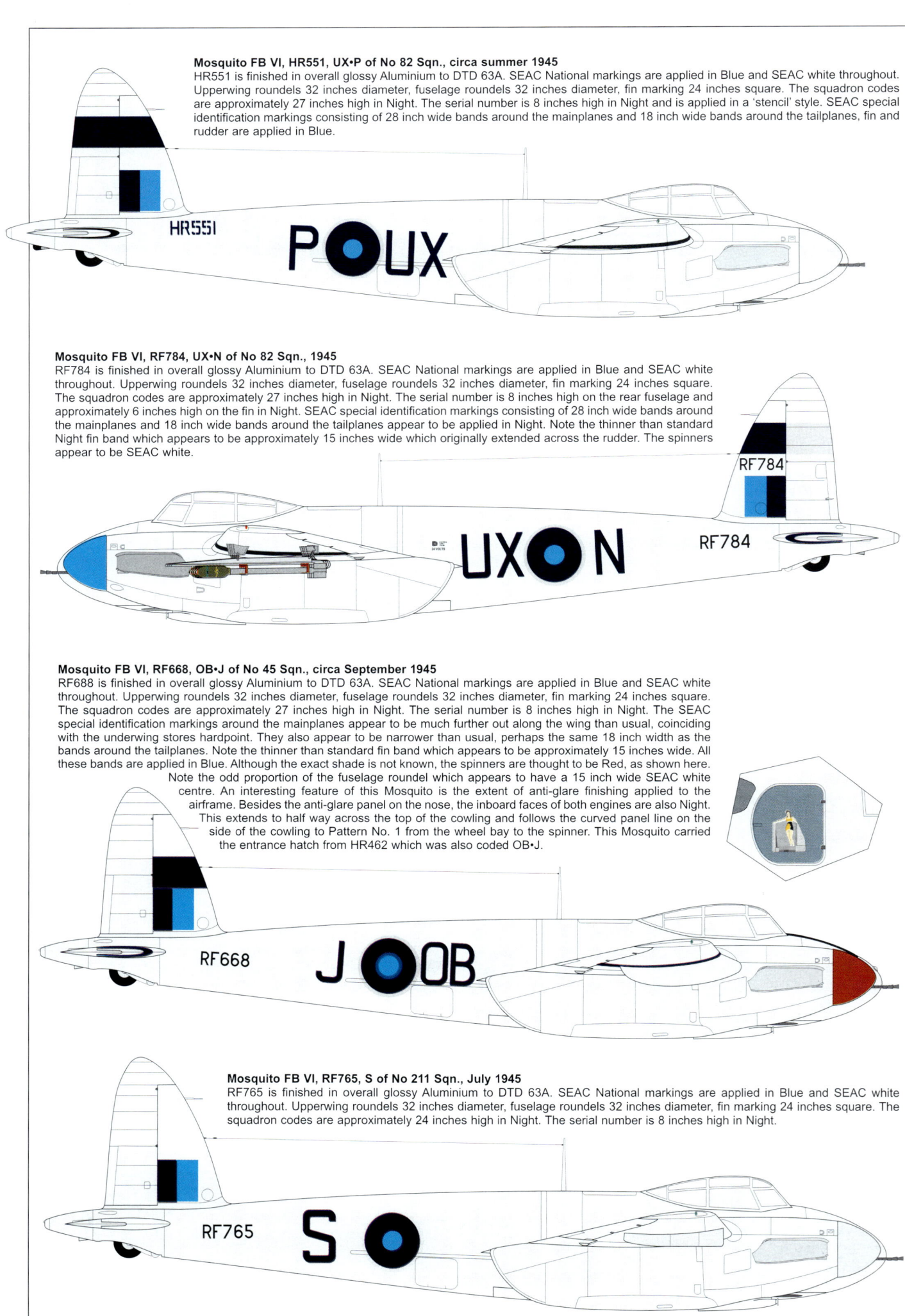

Mosquito FB VI, HR551, UX•P of No 82 Sqn., circa summer 1945
HR551 is finished in overall glossy Aluminium to DTD 63A. SEAC National markings are applied in Blue and SEAC white throughout. Upperwing roundels 32 inches diameter, fuselage roundels 32 inches diameter, fin marking 24 inches square. The squadron codes are approximately 27 inches high in Night. The serial number is 8 inches high in Night and is applied in a 'stencil' style. SEAC special identification markings consisting of 28 inch wide bands around the mainplanes and 18 inch wide bands around the tailplanes, fin and rudder are applied in Blue.

Mosquito FB VI, RF784, UX•N of No 82 Sqn., 1945
RF784 is finished in overall glossy Aluminium to DTD 63A. SEAC National markings are applied in Blue and SEAC white throughout. Upperwing roundels 32 inches diameter, fuselage roundels 32 inches diameter, fin marking 24 inches square. The squadron codes are approximately 27 inches high in Night. The serial number is 8 inches high on the rear fuselage and approximately 6 inches high on the fin in Night. SEAC special identification markings consisting of 28 inch wide bands around the mainplanes and 18 inch wide bands around the tailplanes appear to be applied in Night. Note the thinner than standard Night fin band which appears to be approximately 15 inches wide which originally extended across the rudder. The spinners appear to be SEAC white.

Mosquito FB VI, RF668, OB•J of No 45 Sqn., circa September 1945
RF688 is finished in overall glossy Aluminium to DTD 63A. SEAC National markings are applied in Blue and SEAC white throughout. Upperwing roundels 32 inches diameter, fuselage roundels 32 inches diameter, fin marking 24 inches square. The squadron codes are approximately 27 inches high in Night. The serial number is 8 inches high in Night. The SEAC special identification markings around the mainplanes appear to be much further out along the wing than usual, coinciding with the underwing stores hardpoint. They also appear to be narrower than usual, perhaps the same 18 inch width as the bands around the tailplanes. Note the thinner than standard fin band which appears to be approximately 15 inches wide. All these bands are applied in Blue. Although the exact shade is not known, the spinners are thought to be Red, as shown here. Note the odd proportion of the fuselage roundel which appears to have a 15 inch wide SEAC white centre. An interesting feature of this Mosquito is the extent of anti-glare finishing applied to the airframe. Besides the anti-glare panel on the nose, the inboard faces of both engines are also Night. This extends to half way across the top of the cowling and follows the curved panel line on the side of the cowling to Pattern No. 1 from the wheel bay to the spinner. This Mosquito carried the entrance hatch from HR462 which was also coded OB•J.

Mosquito FB VI, RF765, S of No 211 Sqn., July 1945
RF765 is finished in overall glossy Aluminium to DTD 63A. SEAC National markings are applied in Blue and SEAC white throughout. Upperwing roundels 32 inches diameter, fuselage roundels 32 inches diameter, fin marking 24 inches square. The squadron codes are approximately 24 inches high in Night. The serial number is 8 inches high in Night.

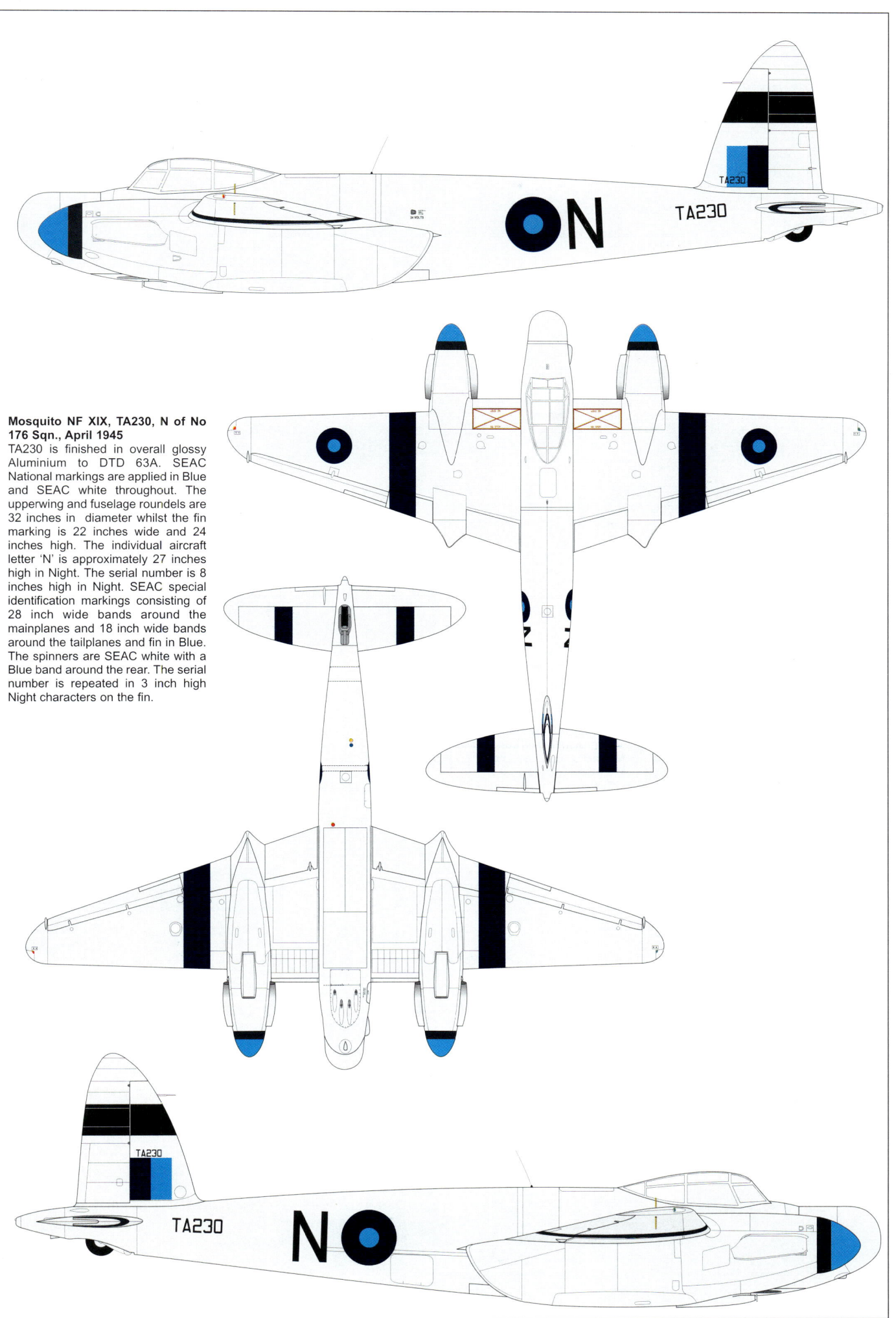

Mosquito NF XIX, TA230, N of No 176 Sqn., April 1945

TA230 is finished in overall glossy Aluminium to DTD 63A. SEAC National markings are applied in Blue and SEAC white throughout. The upperwing and fuselage roundels are 32 inches in diameter whilst the fin marking is 22 inches wide and 24 inches high. The individual aircraft letter 'N' is approximately 27 inches high in Night. The serial number is 8 inches high in Night. SEAC special identification markings consisting of 28 inch wide bands around the mainplanes and 18 inch wide bands around the tailplanes and fin in Blue. The spinners are SEAC white with a Blue band around the rear. The serial number is repeated in 3 inch high Night characters on the fin.

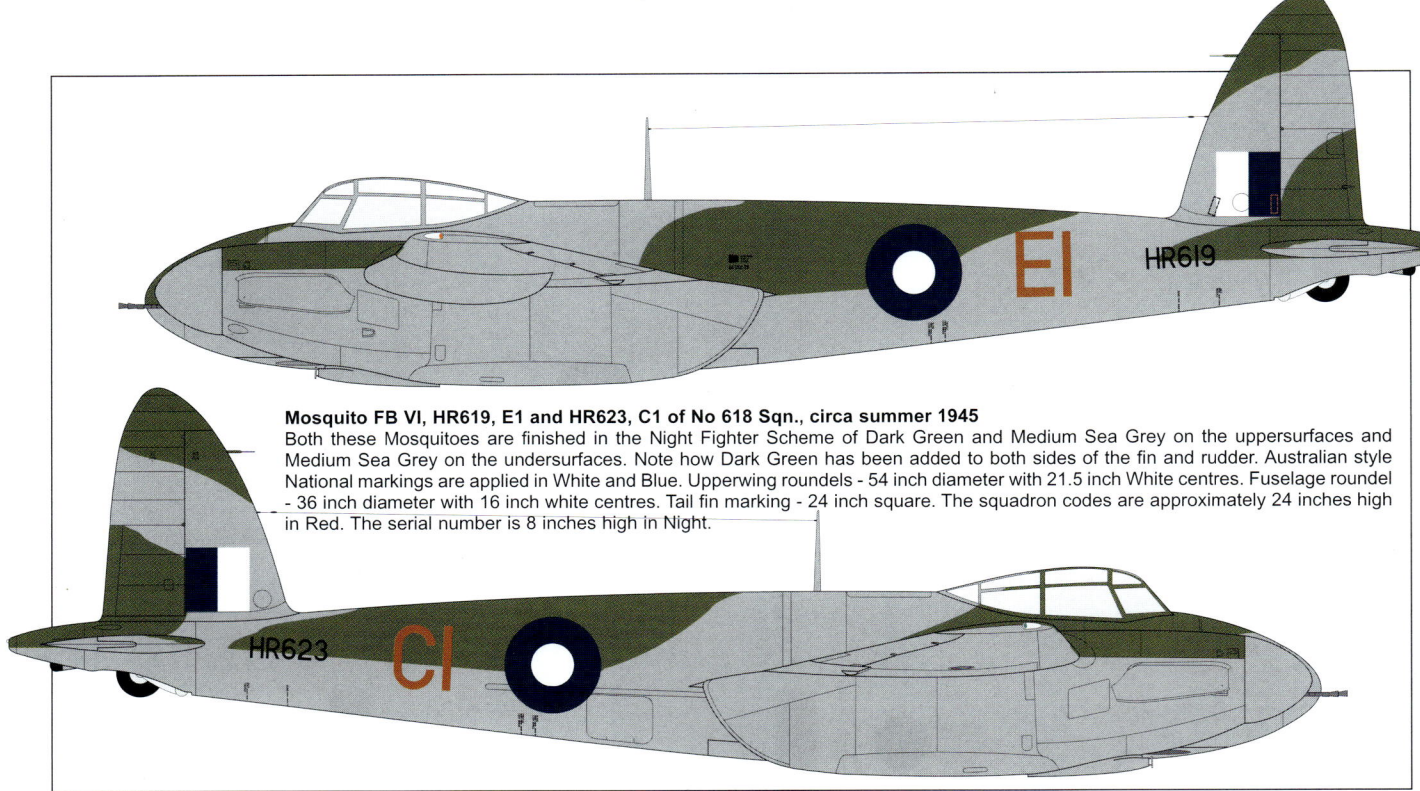

Mosquito FB VI, HR619, E1 and HR623, C1 of No 618 Sqn., circa summer 1945
Both these Mosquitoes are finished in the Night Fighter Scheme of Dark Green and Medium Sea Grey on the uppersurfaces and Medium Sea Grey on the undersurfaces. Note how Dark Green has been added to both sides of the fin and rudder. Australian style National markings are applied in White and Blue. Upperwing roundels - 54 inch diameter with 21.5 inch White centres. Fuselage roundel - 36 inch diameter with 16 inch white centres. Tail fin marking - 24 inch square. The squadron codes are approximately 24 inches high in Red. The serial number is 8 inches high in Night.

However, the Squadron also operated several FB VIs for training purposes, which were not modified to be operated from aboard ship like the B IVs. The FB VI's camouflage scheme was basically the standard Night Fighter Scheme of Dark Green and Medium Sea Grey to which areas of Dark Green camouflage had been added to the fin and rudder. Most, if not all of these Mosquito FB VIs were drawn from a batch of HR-series Standard Motors-built Mosquitoes, manufactured in December 1944, but it is not known for certain whether these extra Dark Green segments of camouflage were applied on the production line or following delivery to the Service.

The FB VI's national markings appear to have been modified in to the RAAF White and Blue type in the same way as the B IVs described in Combat Colours No 5. However, in contrast with the B IVs which only carried an individual aircraft code letter, the FB VIs carried an alphanumeric code, which is thought to have been marked on the aircraft in Red. The origin of this coding system possibly lies in one of two places.

The first possibility is that it is a continuation of the Coastal Command practice of using a number as the squadron code allocated by each station as had been done in the UK following the abandonment of the two letter squadron codes in 1942.

The second possibility is that it was based on a Naval system of identification markings. The Naval system of squadron and individual aircraft identification markings in use in January 1945 was set out in Confidential Admiralty Fleet Order (CAFO) 1901/44 Naval Aircraft Distinguishing Symbols dated 31 August 1944. This stated that there were three forms of Symbol, (a) aircraft attached to Wings or permanently shore based; (b) aircraft attached to A/S Escort Carriers and (c) aircraft not included in either of the above.

As 618 Sqn were not attached to a Naval Wing of any kind and were not based on an Escort Carrier, it would appear that their FB VIs would have fallen into the latter category.

This stated that aircraft were to be marked with a figure-letter or single letter symbol denoting the squadron and individual aircraft, with the symbol being allocated by the parent ship or air station. The numeral '1' which was carried by 618 Squadron's FB VIs could be allocated to either an operational TBR Squadron or a Training Squadron and according to the CAFO was to be marked on operational aircraft, (except A/S aircraft), in Sky; on A/S aircraft in Medium Sea Grey and on training and ancillary aircraft in Yellow.

Whilst this fails to explain why Red appears to have been used, it is of interest to note that the previous CAFO, CAFO 1951/43 dated 16 September 1943, had stated that, 'Aircraft Symbols were to be 'dull red' in colour', and this might go some way to explaining this interesting anomaly.

As in Europe, No 618 Sqn never saw action against the enemy and disbanded at the end of the war in the Far East in August 1945.

Below: Mosquito FB VI, HR609, S1 of 618 Sqn., in Australia in 1945. HR609 is finished in the Night Fighter Scheme of Dark Green and Medium Sea Grey with RAAF style Blue and White national markings. The serial number is Night and the codes are thought to be Red. Why an alpha numeric code was applied only to the Squadron's FB VIs, which were used for training purposes, is unclear. Note the areas of Dark Green camouflage on the fin and rudder. These were a common feature on all the FB VIs shipped out to Australia for use by 618 Sqn.

Mosquito Colours

MAP colours	Closest FS 595B match
Dark Earth	30118
Dark Green	34079
Ocean Grey	36152
Sky Grey	36463
Sky Blue	35550
Sky	34424
Azure Blue	35231
PRU Blue	35189
Medium Sea Grey	36270
Night	37030
Red	30109
White	- - - - -
SEAC white	35488
Blue	35048
Yellow	33538
Extra Dark Sea Grey	36099
Dark Slate Grey	34096
Aluminium	17178